THE BEAST IN THE PULPIT, THE LAMB IN OUR HEARTS

PREACHING THE BOOK OF REVELATION IN MAINLINE CHURCHES TODAY

Upcoming Titles by Rolf Svanoe:

I Love to Preach the Story, Cycle A
I Love to Preach the Story, Cycle B
I Love to Preach the Story, Cycle C
Advent and Lent in Narnia:
A "Fantastic" Worship Series for All Ages

Previous Titles by Rolf Svanoe:

Bread for the Journey

THE BEAST
IN THE PULPIT,
THE LAMB
IN OUR HEARTS

PREACHING THE BOOK OF REVELATION
IN MAINLINE CHURCHES TODAY

Rolf D. Svanoe

CSS Publishing Company, Inc.

Lima, Ohio

The Beast In the Pulpit, The Lamb In Our Heart
FIRST EDITION
Copyright © 2021
by CSS Publishing Co., Inc.

Library of Congress Cataloging-in-Publication Data

Names: Svanoe, Rolf, author.
Title: The beast in the pulpit, the lamb in our hearts : preaching the Book
  of Revelation in mainline churches today / Rolf D. Svanoe.
Description: Lima, Ohio : CSS Publishing Company, Inc., [2022] | Includes
  bibliographical references.
Identifiers: LCCN 2021060502 (print) | LCCN 2021060503 (ebook) | ISBN
  9780788030321 (paperback) | ISBN 9780788030338 (pdf)
Subjects: LCSH: Bible. Revelation--Homiletical use. | Bible.
  Revelation--Sermons. | Bible. Revelation--Criticism, interpretation,
  etc. | Protestant churches--Sermons. | Preaching--United States.
Classification: LCC BS2825.55 .S83 2022 (print) | LCC BS2825.55 (ebook) |
  DDC 228/.06--dc23/eng/20220222
LC record available at https://lccn.loc.gov/2021060502
LC ebook record available at https://lccn.loc.gov/2021060503

For more information about CSS Publishing Company resources, visit our website at www.csspub.com, email us at csr@csspub.com, or call (800) 241-4056.

e-book:
ISBN-13: 978-0-7880-3033-8
ISBN-10: 0-7880-3033-7

ISBN-13: 978-0-7880-3032-1
ISBN-10: 0-7880-3032-9   ELECTRONICALLY PRINTED

Acknowledgments

My goal in writing this book is to provide a resource for busy pastors to address, in a responsible way, the message in the book of Revelation. There is little in my book that is original. I have simply tried to assemble in one place the insights of many scholars who have thought deeply about this book. What is original are the sermons on Revelation. I don't include them here as examples of "good" sermons. Many of my stories are personal. I simply want to show a way to preach this book that hopefully will encourage pastors to tell their own stories as they craft their sermons.

Much of the material for this book comes from my dissertation work on a Doctor of Ministry in Biblical Preaching degree, which I earned in 2008 from Luther Seminary in St. Paul, Minnesota. The inspiration for my topic came from Professor Craig Koester in his class, Preaching the Book of Revelation. My degree would not have been possible without the encouragement and financial support of the congregation I was serving at the time — Peace Lutheran in Sioux Falls, South Dakota.

Over the last ten years, these ideas have needed time to settle and mature. I am grateful to the people of Greenfield Lutheran in Harmony, Minnesota for their encouragement as we explored this book together in 2018. Reading Revelation again in the context of current events reminded me again just how prophetic and relevant this book really is.

Lastly, I would like to thank my wife, Kimberly Utke Svanoe, a retired college music professor, for her diligence in reading and editing the manuscript.

Contents

The Strange Silence Of Revelation In The Pulpit

"Do Not Seal Up The Words Of The Prophecy Of This Book"

The Revelation of John suffers from both abuse and neglect. In some quarters it is interpreted literally, and badly, in service of particular theological agendas, while in mainline denominations it has been neglected, if not abandoned. The Revelation to John is the sixth largest volume in the New Testament library, but it is seldom preached in mainline pulpits. Many preachers ignore or intentionally avoid it, except at funerals. Revelation is the only book in the Bible that contains a specific promise of blessing for those who read it. "Blessed is the one who reads aloud the words of the prophecy and blessed are those who hear and who keep what is written in it" (Revelation 1:3). Most congregations never hear or receive this blessing. A refrain in the letters to the seven churches is, "Let anyone who has an ear listen to what the Spirit is saying to the churches" (Revelation 2:7, 11, 17, 29, 3:6, 13, 22). But how will congregations listen if preachers continue to neglect this book from the pulpit?

The purpose of this book is to recover the book of Revelation for mainline churches today. Why should mainline pastors spend the time and energy required to understand and preach the book of Revelation? Several reasons warrant this effort. Revelation is part of the canon we regard as the Word of God. Its place in the canon was hard-won. Few books of the Bible have had more influence on the art and music of the church. It is theologically significant. One scholar claims, "Revelation can be seen to be not only one of the finest literary works in the New Testament, but also one of the greatest theological achievements of early

Christianity."[1] And, properly understood, it is relevant. Another scholar has written, "I hope to demystify... what I personally feel is one of the most relevant portions of the New Testament."[2] These are bold claims that deserve to be explored and studied.

In view of such high praise and promise, why have most mainline preachers ignored the book of Revelation? There are many objections to preaching Revelation, some based on its content, and other objections that are external to its message.

Internal Objections to Preaching Revelation

One of the main reasons Revelation is not preached more often is that it is not as intelligible or readily accessible as the gospels or Paul's letters. For many, the book simply does not make sense. The plot is hard to follow. The symbols confound the imagination. How does one picture a beast with seven heads and ten horns? It is almost comical to see how artists have struggled to fit them all on a canvas. The apocalyptic genre is not as familiar or understood as it was in the first century. The symbols confuse and disturb contemporary readers. Revelation's apocalyptic worldview is so alien today and requires so much time and effort to explain that it is simply easier to preach other parts of the Bible. In the task of getting from text to sermon, so much effort must be spent explaining the text that there is little time left for proclamation. Most preachers regard this as boring and counter-productive.

Many are repulsed by the language of violence and suffering in Revelation. D. H Lawrence described Revelation as "the Judas of the New Testament," implying that it is a betrayal of the spirit and teaching of Jesus to love one's enemies.[3] Like Lawrence, many have labeled Revelation theologically inferior. Where is the gracious Savior who forgave his enemies on the cross? What are preachers supposed to do with saints pleading for divine

1 Richard Bauckham, *The Theology of the Book of Revelation*. New Testament Theology (New York: Cambridge University Presss, 1993), 22.
2 Ronald L. Farmer, *Revelation*, ed. Russell Pregeant and David J. Lull. Chalice Commentaires for Today (St. Louis, MO: Chalice Press, 2005), xi.
3 D. H. Lawrence, *Apocalypse* (London: Heinemann, 1931).

vengeance and welcoming God's judgments on their enemies with delight? What preacher wants to explain the martyred saints under the altar, who cry out to God, "How long will it be before you judge and avenge our blood on the inhabitants of the earth?" (Revelation 6:10). God's wrath is vividly portrayed as a huge winepress from which human blood flows as high as a horse's bridle for 200 miles (Revelation 14:20). When the great whore is judged, the multitude in heaven cries out, "Hallelujah! The smoke goes up from her forever and ever" (Revelation 19:3). These scenes are not easy for preachers to handle. It is understandable why some preachers regard Revelation as confusing and theologically suspect, revealing a cruel and vindictive God unworthy of worship.

Another objection many raise against Revelation is its treatment of women. Women are grouped according to their sexual status as virgin, bride, or whore. The 144,000 who have not "defiled themselves with women" (Revelation 14:4) led some to accuse the author, John, of misogyny. At least one commentator maintains that to preach and teach this part of Revelation one must "read against the text."[4] This does not encourage preachers to proclaim Revelation from the pulpit.

Revelation's many scenes of earthly destruction lead some to accuse it of espousing world-negating values. The popular definition of the word "apocalypse" in contemporary culture is synonymous with an end-of-the-world catastrophe. James Watt, former Secretary of the Interior under President Ronald Reagan, was widely criticized for his lack of environmental concern because of his expressed belief in the imminent return of Christ and anticipated destruction of the world.[5] With current concerns about global warming and heightened environmental awareness, is a renewed interest in Revelation justifiable?

4 Greg Carey, "Teaching and Preaching the Book of Revelation in the Church," *Review & Expositor* 98.1 (2001): 97.
5 Jonathan Kirsch, *A History of the End of the World: How the Most Controversial Book in the Bible Changed the Course of Western Civilization* (San Francisco, CA: HarperSanFrancisco, 2006).

Preachers who wander into Revelation's strange landscape will have to come to terms with symbols of judgment and eschatology. Hell, the lake of fire, and the second death are frightening and potent symbols. While references to judgment and hell are not unique to Revelation, they are much harder to avoid here than in the gospels or epistles. Preachers must examine their own beliefs about the afterlife and interpret them from within their own theological traditions.

Finally, there is the matter of Christ's return. One might legitimately conclude that the author of Revelation was simply wrong about Christ's imminent return. The first and penultimate verses are just a few of the many places in the book that announce Christ's expected return. While this expectation is not unique to Revelation, it is particularly problematic in a book filled with eschatological hope. How does the preacher interpret this language responsibly and avoid end-time speculations?

Author Jonathan Kirsch sums up many of these critical concerns:

> Revelation has served as a "language arsenal" in a great many of the social, cultural, and political conflicts in Western history. Again and again, Revelation has stirred some dangerous men and women to act out their own private apocalypses. Above all, the moral calculus of Revelation — the demonization of one's enemies, the sanctification of revenge taking, and the notion that history must end in catastrophe — can be detected in some of the worst atrocities and excesses of every age, including our own.

> For all of these reasons, the rest of us ignore the book of Revelation only at our impoverishment and, more to the point, at our own peril.[6]

These are the concerns that modern preachers must deal with and interpret for their congregations in a theologically responsible way.

6 Ibid, 18.

While many homiletical pitfalls exist within the message of Revelation itself, it should also be said that the book enjoys growing interest in the culture. Rather than rail against dispensationalist interpretations, the challenge for the wise preacher is to propose a better understanding of Revelation and hopefully present its great themes and messages in ways that are both compelling and faithful.

External Objections to Preaching Revelation

A preacher wishing to spend more time in the book of Revelation will get little help from the lectionary. Revelation makes a limited appearance in the Revised Common Lectionary, appearing only twelve times in the three-year cycle.[7] As a result, in churches committed to following the lectionary, Revelation has little presence. One of the touted benefits of using a three-year lectionary is to expose congregations to the whole counsel of God. The lectionary forces preachers into homiletical territory they might not personally choose. Apparently, the architects of the lectionary assumed there is much counsel in Revelation that contemporary churches do not need to hear, at least not from the pulpit in worship. Instead of encouraging homiletical choices from Revelation, the lectionary committee apparently held the view that Revelation should be avoided in the pulpit. Perhaps the confusing language and symbols of Revelation are better reserved for Bible study, where questions and answers can help to clarify the meaning.

The few times that Revelation does appear in the lectionary offer a truncated view of its message. The series of lections for Easter C, highlight the comforting visions of heaven. These texts are appropriately chosen for the Easter season and the proclamation of Christ's victory over death. They contain the most accessible language in Revelation, and some of the most comforting and hopeful passages in the Bible. Pastors often

7 Six appearances are in the Easter season year C (Revelation 1:4-8; 5:11-14; 7:9-17; 21:1-6; 21:10, 22-22:5; 22:12-14, 16-17, 20-21). Additional lections from Revelation are appointed for All Saints AB, Christ the King B, and New Year ABC.

preach from these texts at funerals. But these lections avoid the more confusing passages that lie at the heart of its message, a message that gives unique insight into the nature of evil, with a call for the church to repent and resist that evil. This becomes blatantly clear on Easter 7C when the lectionary editors go to great lengths to avoid any language of judgment. The appointed lection is Revelation 22:12-14, 16-17, 20-21. In each case in which the lection has been interrupted, all language of judgment or warning has been edited out. This emasculation of the text is like skipping Good Friday and going directly from Palm Sunday to Easter. Straining to avoid any "negative" language, the heart of Revelation's message has been missed. The lectionary editors have done exactly what John warned against. "If anyone takes away from the words of the book of this prophecy, God will take away that person's share in the tree of life and in the holy city, which are described in this book" (Revelation 22:19). The promised blessing for the hearer is missed by not engaging the book in its entirety.

Another external reason why Revelation is not preached more often involves seminary training. Most pastors received little or no formal training in preaching apocalyptic texts. This becomes one more subject to fit into an already crowded curriculum. Seminaries are beginning to rectify this omission. With new research into the book of Revelation and increasing interest in apocalyptic themes in the culture, some seminaries are making greater room for the study of eschatology. For pastors untrained in apocalyptic literature, the effort required to understand and preach these texts is so formidable that more accessible parts of the Bible are often chosen for the sermon.

Some preachers are simply ignorant of Revelation's message and relevance. They were told once that Revelation was written to an oppressed community in need of a message of hope and comfort. They wonder what message Revelation could possibly speak to the wealthy and comfortable churches they serve, except of course at a funeral.

Many preachers have cultivated the habit of preaching on the gospel lesson every week. By design, the gospel lesson intentionally dominates the liturgy. Congregations are invited to stand at its reading. Even calling it the "Holy Gospel" implies that the other lessons read in worship are somehow less important. The book of Revelation suffers the same fate the Old Testament does in many pulpits. Additionally, the book of Revelation has a public relations problem: the impression exists that much preaching on Revelation (past and present) is of the "fire and brimstone" variety. Most mainline preachers gladly avoid it and choose the gospel lesson.

While a great deal of interest exists in congregations concerning Revelation, much of what people know about it comes from pop culture or from end-time forecasters like the *Left Behind* series.[8] Though many pastors regard such interpretations of Revelation as misguided or even dangerous, they lack a coherent alternative to present to their congregations. Many pastors have members who have read and loved the *Left Behind* series, and while these members may acknowledge the novels as fiction, they seem to embrace or accept the underlying interpretive presuppositions as authoritative. Pastors may not want the challenge of arguing with their members who have embraced these dispensationalist frameworks. To overcome this requires time, study, patience, and knowledge. Most pastors are not willing to spend their energies in this way and instead opt for silence.

Some pastors view Revelation as militaristic or imperialistic. They reject the use of end time scenarios to justify political and militaristic purposes. For example, when former President Ronald Reagan professed a belief in a battle of Armageddon that would take place in Israel, one wonders to what extent these prophetic interpretations actually impact foreign policy. Or, when Israel invaded Lebanon recently, premillennial dispensationalists speculated whether such action would usher in the final battle of Armageddon and the return of Christ. Many news commentators repeat this edgy language, which stimulates interest and promotes the news. Most mainline preachers do not want to add to the confusion or contribute to further misinformation and, therefore,

8 Tim LaHaye and Jerry Jenkins, *Left Behind: A Novel of the Earth's Last Days* (Wheaton, IL: Tyndale House Publishers, 1996).

leave the book of Revelation to others in the belief that "the less said, the better."

Reasons to Preach Revelation

On September 11, 2001, people looked at the burning towers and called on the language of "apocalypse" to describe what they were experiencing. The same thing happened after the Christmas Tsunami in 2004 and Hurricane Katrina in 2005. When former Vice President Al Gore presented his case for global warming and warned that we have ten years to turn the environment around, people used apocalyptic or end time categories. The word "apocalypse" has been co-opted by contemporary culture to refer to disastrous end-of-the-world scenarios. This is a distortion that must be corrected. Gail R. O'Day has written that "most contemporary Christians' presuppositions about Revelation are shaped more by popular culture than by the traditions of the church that have evolved over centuries of Christian practice."[9] One only needs to do a Google search on the word "apocalypse" to discover a tremendous presence and interest in Revelation. People are fascinated by the book, both inside and outside the faith community. The church, therefore, does its members a disservice when it remains silent. Preachers need to reclaim the book of Revelation by giving it the same serious attention they give any other book of the Bible. Some would say that the church needs to give Revelation *more* attention in order to rehabilitate its poor reputation and overcome the mistakes and prejudices that hold it hostage.

When horrors strike our world today, when tsunamis drown thousands, or wildfires rage unchecked, when millions perish through genocide or ethnic cleansing, it is the book of Revelation that can offer a theological framework for understanding the worst about our world. More than any other book of the Bible, Revelation calls the church to resist evil through its faithful witness to the truth. Precisely because Revelation understands

9 Gail R. O'Day, "Teaching and Preaching the Book of Revelation," *Word & World* 25.3 (2005): 247.

the nature of evil so clearly, it can also offer a powerful word of hope in God's ongoing love and faithfulness. A thoughtful interpretation of the book can greatly benefit the people of God.

While many are reluctant to preach from Revelation, others passionately believe that the message of this book is exactly what first-world Christians, seduced by modern forms of idolatry, need to hear:

> Daily we are invited to worship at the altars of consumerism, to champion the expansion of an empire of global capital, to seek security behind walls of military might, to pursue ideals of greed and selfishness at the cost of environmental degradation and destruction. Like John's audience we are increasingly faced with a choice — to be citizens who participate in empire blithely uncritical or studiously unconscious of the suffering it daily unleashes on the world, or to seek a more costly way in testimony to an alternative construction of our social and planetary order. If there were ever a biblical writing that urged a critical appraisal of society, Revelation is surely the one. If there were ever a time for Christians to think critically about empire and its costs, it is now. Revelation is the book of the hour.[10]

The book of Revelation invites us to think critically about empire, and Christians' participation in a world that often conflicts with biblical values.

It is a testimony to the power and inspiration of scripture that it continues to speak a prophetic word in new times and places. This prophetic word is what many commentators feel compelled to give voice to today:

> The book of Revelation offers a passionate critique of the oppressive political, economic, social and religious realities of the Roman Empire. It also

10 Harry O. Maier, *Apocalypse Recalled: The Book of Revelation after Christendom* (Minneapolis, MN: Fortress Press, 2002), xi.

unveils the vision of a world-in-the-making, a vision of justice and peace embodied in a new heaven, a new earth, and a new Jerusalem. And it delivers a rhetorically charged challenge for believers to withdraw from the Empire and to live even now in the worship and service of the God who is making all things new... [to] oppose oppression in all its forms in our world, and express the longing to create a world free of injustice, racism, patriarchy, destruction of the environment, economic exploitation, and empire.[11]

The Revelation to John has a much-needed prophetic message for North American churches, as well as to people outside the church. It is important to present a compelling alternative to popular dispensationalist end-time scenarios, as represented in the *Left Behind* books and movies. These interpretive frameworks are foreign to the book of Revelation, and rely on selective proof texts. When Revelation is interpreted as a whole, it offers a compelling grand narrative that makes sense of the world as it is and offers a vision of hope for what the world can be. Its ancient images come to life and have the potential for speaking powerfully to our contemporary world.

Epic narratives are increasingly popular in society today. Books and movies like *The Lord of the Rings* or *Star Wars* create alternative worlds filled with frightening symbols that ultimately end in a joyous resolution. Exploring the book of Revelation gives the church an opportunity to use similar media in proclaiming its alternative vision for our world. Author Kathleen Norris has echoed Revelation's powerful use of language:

> This is a poet's book, which is probably the best argument for reclaiming it from fundamentalists. It doesn't tell, it shows, over and over again, its images unfolding, pushing hard against the limits

11 David Rhoads, "Introduction," In *From Every People and Nation: The Book of Revelation in Intercultural Perspective*, ed. David Rhoads. (Minneapolis, MN: Augsburg Fortress Press, 2005), 1.

of language and metaphor, engaging the listener in a tale that has the satisfying yet unsettling logic of a dream.[12]

Perhaps more than any other book in the Bible, Revelation's powerful use of language can speak today in ways that capture the contemporary imagination.

For many years the dominant lens through which scholars interpreted the apocalypse was that it was written to a church undergoing intense persecution. That view has been heavily revised in the last thirty years. Current scholarship believes that the original audience of Revelation was much more diverse. There certainly were those persecuted because of their faith in Jesus, but there were also those trying to remain faithful amidst the pressure to assimilate into the dominant Roman culture. Some Christians were complacent, comfortable and wealthy. The diverse audience for the book, as exemplified in the seven churches in Revelation 2-3, is reflective of the diversity we find in our churches today. The challenge for the preacher is to help make those connections between the ancient world and our world, and allow the book to speak a prophetic message today.

12 Kathleen Norris, "Introduction," In *Revelation*, ed. Will Self, Pocket Canon Series. (New York: Grove Press, 1999), 11.

A Theology Of Preaching The Book Of Revelation

"The Testimony Of Jesus Is The Spirit Of Prophecy"

I used to live in Harmony, Minnesota. Harmony is located about 25 miles from Spring Grove to the east, and 25 miles from Spring Valley to the west. When I first moved there, I was always getting those two towns mixed up. One day I had a meeting in Spring Grove and ended up in Spring Valley, the exact wrong direction. The problem began in my assumptions thinking that I knew where to go, but I found out that I had ended up in the wrong place. I wonder if many preachers don't approach the book of Revelation that way? Our starting assumptions will determine where we end up, and if our assumptions are wrong so will our interpretation.

Preaching the book of Revelation is, in some ways, no different than preaching any other book of the Bible. A good place to begin is with the question, "How does one preach any biblical text?" Discovering the meaning of a text has, in the previous century, relied largely on the historical-critical method. In his essay on biblical theology in *The Interpreter's Dictionary of the Bible*, Krister Stendahl set the basic ground rule: first find out what the text meant when it was written, and then ask what the text means today.[13] In other words, if one can successfully determine what the text meant, one is more likely to faithfully discern what the text means today.

Biblical preaching has taken different forms over the years. In one model, the preacher is like a treasure hunter. The goal is to find the central thought or idea in the historical text, decode it, and then deliver it to the contemporary hearers in terms they

13 Krister Stendahl, "Biblical Theology, Contemporary," In *The Interpreter's Dictionary of the Bible*, ed. George Buttrick, et al. (Nashville: Abingdon, 1962), 418-432.

can understand. This is a teaching model designed to change the listener's thinking. The preacher's task is to discern the main thought or point and then teach it in a way that people can apply to their lives. A second model of biblical preaching focuses more on the experience in the text. The preacher's task is to discover the experience of the original hearers, their sense of joy, loss, grief, or hope, and then apply that to similar experiences of today. A third model for biblical preaching does not try to duplicate the thought or experience in the text, but rather the eventfulness or the results of the text. For example, what happened to the reader as he or she encountered the passage? How can the sermon do the same? How can the sermon help listeners have the same encounter with the living God?

All three of these perspectives for understanding biblical preaching are helpful when it comes to the book of Revelation. Revelation's images and symbols speak to hearers on multiple levels. Rather than being code language meant to sneak a message past imperial censors, the images function more to reveal and open up worlds of meaning that ordinary language simply cannot. Revelation's symbols speak not only to the mind, but also to the heart and soul. To hear the book of Revelation read aloud is a profound experience, an aural "unveiling" of God, ourselves and the world in which we live.

Biblical preaching is more than simply an encounter with a biblical text. In proclaiming the text, preachers do so with the conviction that God has promised to speak through the sermon to God's people. "Though we use the Bible, we do not preach so that people may encounter the Bible, but so that people may encounter Christ."[14] The goal of the sermon, ultimately, is to help people grow in their relationship with God.

Preaching the Word of God

Biblical preaching grows out of the conviction that God has acted in history, most clearly in the life, death and resurrection

14 David L. Bartlett, *Between the Bible and the Church: New Methods for Biblical Preaching* (Nashville: Abingdon Press, 1999), 13.

of Jesus Christ. Jesus Christ is God's Word to the world. "In the beginning was the word, and the word was with God, and the word was God" (John 1:1). "Long ago God spoke to our ancestors in many and various ways by the prophets, but in these last days he has spoken to us by a Son…" (Hebrews 1:1-2). God has spoken a word to the world, and that word is Jesus. Preaching is first and foremost the proclamation of Jesus Christ as God's preeminent word to the world. While that word will certainly contain details of Jesus' life, ethical teaching, moral example, and miracles, that word will find its center and primary authority in the cross. "For I decided to know nothing among you except Jesus Christ, and him crucified" (1 Corinthians 2:2). It is in Christ on the cross that God's nature and identity is most clearly revealed.

Locating the theological center of the Bible and proclamation in the crucified Christ, in a theology of the cross, is precisely what the author of the book of Revelation does. The dominant image for Christ in Revelation is that of the "Lamb standing as if it had been slaughtered" (Revelation 5:6). The word, 'lamb,' referring to Christ, occurs 28 times. Christ's role in Revelation is to establish God's kingdom on earth. But Christ does not do this through military conquest. Christ wins a victory over evil through his death and resurrection. "The continuing and ultimate victory of God over evil which the rest of Revelation describes is no more than the working-out of the decisive victory of the Lamb on the cross."[15] New Testament scholar Barbara Rossing described Revelation's central theological focus:

> From beginning to end, Revelation's vision of the lamb teaches a "theology of the cross," of God's power made manifest in weakness, similar to Paul's theology of the cross in First Corinthians. Lamb theology is the whole message of Revelation. Evil is defeated not by overwhelming force or violence but by the lamb's suffering love on the cross. The victim becomes the victor.[16]

15 Bauckham, *The Theology of the Book of Revelation*, 75.
16 Barbara R. Rossing, *The Rapture Exposed: The Message of Hope in the Book of Revelation* (Boulder, CO: Westview Press, 2004), 111.

This theology of the cross is also the way in which Revelation calls the church to conquer by following the lamb and participating in his death and resurrection. "John's prophecy is initially a revelation to the churches of the role they are to play as prophetic witnesses to the nations ...that their faithful witness and death is to be instrumental in the conversion of the nations of the world."[17] If a theology of the cross is the central interpretive lens for understanding the book of Revelation, it follows that this theology also needs to be at the center of the church's preaching from this book.

Biblical preaching not only proclaims the crucified and risen Christ, but it does so *through* a biblical text. According to Martin Luther, the Bible is the cradle which contains the Christ. It is through the words of the Bible that we encounter the living Christ. It is in this sense that we call the Bible the Word of God. Because of its primary witness to the events of salvation history, the Bible has a unique place and authority. For this reason it is the "norm of norms" for faith and life. "All scripture is inspired by God and is useful for teaching, for reproof, for correction, and for training in righteousness" (2 Timothy 3:16).

In the first four centuries after Jesus' resurrection, the church developed the canon of scripture. This lengthy process determined the documents it considered inspired and authoritative witnesses to Christ. As it lived with these writings, the church, in deliberation and discernment, determined which were "useful" or not. The writings that fostered a relationship with the living Christ were accepted into the canon. Those that did not were rejected. But it was the church that made that decision. So, in one sense, the authority of scripture is an authority given it by the church. In another sense, the authority of the Bible is given it by God. The Bible is "inspired" by God, not because God dictated it word for word, but because it points to Jesus Christ. It is because of this authority that we call the Bible the word of God.

The third way we speak of the word of God is when a biblical text is proclaimed and heard in the preaching event so that faith

17 Bauckham, *The Theology of the Book of Revelation*, 83-4.

is awakened in the hearts of believers. "So faith comes from what is heard, and what is heard comes through the word of Christ" (Romans 10:17). The authority for preaching comes from proclaiming Christ, the Word of God, who is revealed in the words of scripture. The proclamation itself is the word of God in which God's Spirit, through the words of the biblical witness, conveys the continuing significance of Jesus' life, death and resurrection for contemporary hearers. The written word exists to bear the gospel, the proclamation of Christ to each new generation. "Now Jesus did many other signs in the presence of his disciples, which are not written in this book. But these are written so that you may come to believe that Jesus is the Messiah, the Son of God, and that through believing you may have life in his name" (John 20:30-31). The Bible does not exist so that people will believe in the Bible. The Bible exists so that people may hear the gospel, believe in Jesus Christ, and experience new life in relationship with him. "Preaching lives under the promise that, where the word is faithfully and carefully interpreted, God still speaks to God's people."[18] This conviction guides pastors who step into pulpits week after week.

What is Biblical Preaching?

How does a contemporary preacher preach an ancient text? If one must first understand what it meant before one can understand what it means, where is one to look for that meaning? For years proponents of the historical-critical method assumed that it is possible to discern one objective and universal meaning in a text that applies to all people everywhere. Ironically perhaps, they held this belief even while disagreeing among themselves as to what that one true objective meaning really was. There were, in fact, almost as many interpretations as there were interpreters.

Recently, scholars have moved away from the notion of a single meaning of a text to the possibility of multiple meanings. These meanings may differ in significant ways from each other,

18 Bartlett, *Between the Bible and the Church: New Methods for Biblical Preaching*, 12.

and yet be valid and legitimate interpretations of a text. The question now is not which interpretation is right and which is wrong, but which interpretation helps a community to faithfully hear the gospel?

One can look for the meaning of a text in at least four places. Interpreters search for meaning in the world "behind" the text, the world "in" the text, the world "around" the text, and the world "in front of" the text.[19]

Finding Meaning in the World "Behind" the Text

The world behind any text refers to the historical context in which it was first written. What are the historical characteristics of this text? The tools of the historical-critical method are primary in discovering this world. Source criticism, form criticism, and redaction criticism may be useful to reveal layers of meaning in the text. The social sciences have helped us understand the complex social and economic structures that underlie a biblical text. They also help us understand the sociology of knowledge. What did ordinary people in biblical times know and believe about their world? What did words mean within that particular worldview, and how does that impact our interpretation of the text? More importantly, how does this influence the preaching of the text? "For preaching, the value of the sociological models is not in what they tell us about sociology. First, it is what they tell us about the texts; second, it is what they tell us about the nature of the biblical communities out of which the texts arose."[20] Realizing that the biblical authors shaped their writings to speak to specific social contexts will encourage discerning preachers to interpret those texts for the social context of Christians today.

Seeking to understand the world behind the text is particularly important when it comes to interpreting apocalyptic texts. The bizarre language and imagery is hard to interpret apart from its original context and meaning. By anchoring apocalyptic texts solidly in the historical setting for which they were written, one

19 David J. Lose, "What Does This Mean? A Four-Part Exercise in Reading Mark 9:2-9 (Transfiguration)," *Word & World* 23.1 (2003).
20 Bartlett, *Between the Bible and the Church: New Methods for Biblical Preaching*, 88.

avoids all kinds of misinterpretations and homiletical misuses of the text. One scholar who can help preachers with this basic approach is Steven Friesen. In *Imperial Cults and the Apocalypse of John: Reading Revelation in the Ruins*, Friesen examined both the archaeological evidence and the text of Revelation in depth. He argues that a detailed analysis of first-century imperial cults in Asia Minor gives us insight into John's criticism of the dominant values of his society.

Another representative study seeking to understand the world behind the text is the book *Unveiling Empire: Reading Revelation Then and Now*, by authors Wes Howard-Brook and Anthony Gwyther. They argued that at the time Revelation was written, Imperial Rome offered its subjects a coherent and ordered structure of reality that brought together the various religious, social, economic and political parts of their world. Crucial to understanding Revelation is an investigation of this historical context. "One of the limitations of many popular works on Revelation is that they do not sufficiently situate the text within the social and historical context out of which John of Patmos's visions took place and were written down."[21] Investigating that historical context will include many things:

> The historical context of the communities requires an examination of how life was lived in the cities of this Roman province. This will involve an exploration of the politics, economics, culture, and mythology of the Roman Empire, particularly as these were found in the Roman province of Asia. As in any society, these elements of the Roman world were not separate realities. Rather, together they constituted a social totality that was interwoven in a web of imperial power. These were the avenues by which Rome held the great and the small, the rich and poor, the slave and free in its orbit.[22]

21 Wes Howard-Brook and Anthony Gwyther, *Unveiling Empire: Reading Revelation Then and Now*. The Bible & Liberation Series (Maryknoll, NY: Orbis Books, 1999), xix.
22 Ibid, 89.

Understanding the historical social context helps us understand how radical Revelation's critique of the dominant Roman ideology was, and how its alternative view of reality subverted Roman claims.

Finding Meaning in the World "In" the Text

One of the problems with the historical-critical method is that it takes the Bible out of the hands of ordinary readers who feel incompetent to interpret it. They rely on the experts or professional commentators to tell them what it means. This method takes the texts apart but does not show the reader how to reassemble them. In the last third of the twentieth century, a reappraisal and criticism of this highly analytical method has developed.

A new school of study has emerged that encourages people not to look behind the text, as a window into historical layers of meaning, but to look at the text itself as a finished work of art. On this view, meaning is not something discovered in ancient history; rather, meaning is discovered in the very act of reading and in the effect a text has on the reader. This method of interpretation pays attention to the literary dimensions of a passage.

Crucial to understanding a text is to locate it within its literary context as part of a larger narrative. On this view, narrative or literary criticism becomes the primary tool for interpretation. Such elements as plot, character development and dialogue help reveal the meaning in the text. For preachers, this means that our sermons will not only be shaped by the pericope selected for that Sunday, but also shaped by its context in a larger narrative.

David Barr has championed this method of interpreting Revelation. He explains the reasons many people today fail to see Revelation as story:

> Because it is part of the Bible, because it is used in our culture to advocate political agendas both of the left and right, because it utilizes an obscure set of images and ideas, because it is all divided up into neat chapters and discrete verses, because we are so familiar with a few of its symbols (such as the

four horsemen or 666), it is easy to miss the most important thing for understanding the Apocalypse: it is a narrative.... Rather than seeking its relation to history or its presumed views of the end-time, we seek its story.... The Apocalypse is in its most basic sense a retelling of the story of Jesus in a new way and with new images.

If we fail to recognize that this is the gospel story, it is because it does not come in gospel form. It is a different kind of literature.[23]

Barr is interested in exploring those things that help people hear Revelation as a story. His prologue explores those "minimal preliminaries" that allow listeners and readers to experience its narrative power, such as content, form, structure and plot, characterization, symbolization and setting. Barr is aware that when people experience a story, they construct their own meaning. His goal is not to tell people what the story means, but to help them make interpretations that are grounded in what the text actually says. That is the principle for adjudicating wildly divergent interpretations. "All interpretations are partial and fragmentary, however, and thus to some degree wrong. But some are more partial, more faulty, more wrong, than others. Or to be positive, some interpretations are more authentic than others."[24] Barr is clear that not all interpretations are to be accepted as equally valid.

How does one preach Revelation from a narrative perspective? This is the subject of Charles Campbell's essay, *Apocalypse Now: Preaching Revelation as Narrative*. Regarding the Revelation narrative, Campbell asserted:

The primary story of Revelation is the story of Jesus. This particular story of the crucified, resurrected, and enthroned lamb shapes the

23 David L. Barr, *Tales of the End: A Narrative Commentary on the Book of Revelation* (Santa Rosa, CA: Polebridge Press, 1998), 1-3.
24 Ibid, 22.

Apocalypse and provides the 'counter story' that subverts and challenges the myths of empire.... Narrative preaching from the Book of Revelation will proclaim the particular story of Jesus as the counter story to the myths of empire in order to empower the community's resistance to the powers of death.[25]

Telling the story of Jesus is the primary task of Revelation.

This narrative style of preaching will be characterized not by telling simplistic stories, but by making deep and repeated connections to the story of Jesus, the lamb that was slain:

Narrative preaching, as I have depicted it, is thus not confined merely to storytelling or homiletical plots. Rather, it is preaching grounded in the story of Jesus and shaped by a narrative logic. Although such narrative preaching may include stories and involve aspects of plot (disequilibrium, reversal, resolution), it is not limited to these formal characteristics, but rather embodies narrative — specifically the story of Jesus — at a deeper level of content and logic.[26]

The flow and direction of the sermon will take its basic shape from the narrative flow and direction of the text.

Finding Meaning in the World "Around" the Text

The world around the text refers to the history of interpretation, the cluster of meaning that the church has given the text through the ages. The Bible is, after all, the church's book, even though parts of it have taken on a life of their own in popular culture. What have Christians been saying about this book for over two thousand years? The history of interpretation and how the church has interpreted a passage reveals, in part, what the text means.

25 Charles L Campbell, "Apocalypse Now: Preaching Revelation as Narrative," In *Narrative Reading, Narrative Preaching: Reuniting New Testament Interpretation and Proclamation*, ed. Joel B. Green and Michael Pasquarello (Grand Rapids, MI: Baker Academic, 2003), 165.
26 Ibid, 167.

This context around the text includes not only its place in the canon and history of interpretation, but also its place in liturgy and church calendar, in word and sacrament, in hymnody and art. One might also add that, when considering Revelation, the world around the text is also its place in popular culture and its history of misuse.

An example of this interpretive focus is the commentary on Revelation by Judith Kovacs and Christopher Rowland.[27] They argue that the reception history of a text is just as significant a window into its meaning as the original context. "An exposition of the Apocalypse that concentrates exclusively on the question 'What did this verse mean?' may miss the distinctive insight offered by later visionaries, who are inspired by the text to new imaginative insights or prophetic pronouncements."[28] Kovacs and Rowland skillfully traced the long and diverse history of interpretation of Revelation not only among theologians, but also among writers, artists, musicians, political figures and visionaries. In a section called, "A Hermeneutical Postscript: Evaluating the Readings," they addressed the question of how one is to judge among the vastly different interpretations of the book that have developed over the years:

> Ultimately, the question of how to adjudicate among varying readings belongs to the interpretative community. Within the Christian community, viewed in the broadest sense, what has been primarily determinative in making sense of the disparate collection we know as the Bible has been the fourfold story of Jesus.... The gospel stories constitute the framework for understanding what counts as faithfulness to Jesus.... Christian faith is given shape by the gospels, not by the epistles (or for that matter the Apocalypse).

27 Judith Kovacs and Christopher Rowland, *Revelation: The Apocalypse of Jesus Christ*, Blackwell Bible Commentaries (Malden, MA: Blackwell Publishing, 2004).
28 Ibid, 13.

If one were to expound the Apocalypse in such a way that its images led to a practice at odds with the pattern of Jesus' life, death and resurrection as found in the gospels, there would be an incompatibility with the gospel…. The witness of Jesus in life and death is evident in the Apocalypse and must pervade interpretations of it. A Christian reading of the Apocalypse has its key in the person of Christ, the lamb in the midst of the divine throne, standing as if it had been slaughtered.[29]

While the church looks for meaning in the history of interpretation of a text, it does not do so uncritically, but always filtered through its theological interpretation of the gospel.

Finding Meaning in the World "In Front of" the Text

Preachers interpret texts within the worldview they inhabit. When it comes to hermeneutics, there is no neutral place to stand. Maintaining "objectivity" when it comes to interpretation is an impossibility. People read from within their social and historical locations. They come to the text with presuppositions, both acknowledged and unacknowledged, and with prejudices and interests. They interpret the text out of their reality and experience. This reality includes such things as gender, majority/minority status, and first world/third world location. The complex task of interpretation is to humbly recognize and honestly name these realities in ourselves and in others.

For full disclosure, allow me to identify my own social location from which I interpret and preach. I am a white male, married with three adult children, living in the upper Midwest of the United States of America. For thirty-five years I have been a pastor in the Evangelical Lutheran Church in America. My interpretive presuppositions are grounded in a theology of the cross, that God is most fully known in Christ's death and resurrection. In this event we learn the truth about the human condition and of

29 Ibid, 248-9.

God's response to our condition. This theological lens functions as the critical norm through which I read and make sense of any passage of scripture.

When presuppositions are identified and named, one can more easily acknowledge that others may interpret texts quite differently. Similarly, when interpreters acknowledge the distance between our world and the world of scripture, they can more easily acknowledge the distance between themselves and contemporaries interpreting out of a different social reality.

A first world theologian who tried to provide a forum for many different cultural readings of Revelation was David Rhoads. In his book, *From Every Tribe and Nation: The Book of Revelation in Intercultural Perspective*, Rhoads stated that his purpose was to give a voice to biblical scholars and theologians from different cultural contexts as they interpreted the book of Revelation for our time. He wrote:

> Encountering interpretations from diverse cultural/social locations can be a startling experience. It can transform the way people understand the Bible, the way they see their own interpretations, and the way they appropriate the Bible for their own life and cultural context. The experience can also empower people to clarify their own cultural location and thereby find their distinctive voice in reading and interpreting the Bible. And, most important, it can enable people to find solidarity with others who share passion and commitment for a new world.[30]

People have read Revelation from a wide variety of contemporary social contexts. Allan Boesak interpreted Revelation in the context of South African apartheid. Pablo Richard read Revelation in light of his experiences in Central America. Tina Pippin, Elisabeth Schüssler Fiorenza and Adela Yarbro Collins all read Revelation from various feminist perspectives. Cultural location influences how people interpret biblical passages.

30 Rhoads, "Introduction." 1-2.

Professor Brian Blount offered a similar observation in his book on Revelation from the African American perspective. "A cultural reading of the Apocalypse not only brings new light to *our* understanding of Revelation; it does so in a way that appreciates how communal groups different from our own will draw their own culturally derived meaning conclusions. It subsequently fosters communication between us and them."[31] Respect for the interpretations of other communities can be an important way to gain new insight into a text.

One must ask, however, whether this means that all readings of Revelation are accurate and equally valid. From a cultural studies perspective, Blount argued in the following passage that the case is always open:

> We never really learn, in that case, which reading is the one objective and correct one. We learn instead how to comprehend the meaning of the text in vastly different and perhaps larger ways because we see and hear how others in their contextual situations access its meaning potential …that doesn't mean the text can be made to mean anything. In intercommunal conversation, the tension that arises between interpreters sharpens focus on the text and brings challenge to damaging, unsavory, and untenable readings. But such concluding challenges are not reached through an appeal to an arbitrary, standard, correct, and objective truth; they are reached in the crucible of communal conflict and conversation.[32]

The role of the community is the hermeneutical key in establishing those interpretive limits.

Another distinctive social location from which to read Revelation is practiced by persons experiencing disease, physical handicap, or mental illness. Marva Dawn wrote her commentary on Revelation as one who has learned weakness from her physical

31 Brian K. Blount, *Can I Get a Witness: Reading Revelation through African American Culture* (Louisville, KY: Westminster John Knox Press, 2005), 5.
32 Ibid, 35.

handicaps and debilitating disease. She found in Revelation a theology of weakness that could offer a gift of hope to Christians today.[33]

Contemporary preachers can benefit from listening to the voices of those interpreting Revelation from diverse perspectives. In looking for meaning in the world "in front of" the text, they will also need to be clear about their own social location and that of their congregation. Preachers need to interpret their parishioners as well as the scripture. In the lively interplay between the two, new and unexpected dimensions of meaning inspired by the Spirit may come alive.

Revelation as Example of Early Christian Preaching

The fact that Revelation is often referred to as a "book" of the Bible obscures the fact that it is an example of early Christian preaching. John was not writing a book to be included in the Bible. He was writing a letter to Christians he knew and with whom he had a pastoral relationship. His letter was not intended for private reading or study, dissected into chapter and verse. John's letter was intended to be read aloud in the worship services of the churches he knew in Asia. The congregations would have gathered for praise and prayer, and listened to the letter as it was read by the worship leader, followed by a celebration of the Eucharist. "Blessed is the one who reads aloud the words of the prophecy, and blessed are those who hear and who keep what is written in it" (Revelation 1:3).

From the start, Revelation itself claims to be Christian prophecy. This claim is repeated at the end of the book as well in 22:7, 10, 18-19. Richard Bauckham identified two different kinds of prophecy in the early Christian church: *oracles*, that the prophet spoke in the name of God or Christ, and *reports of visions*, that the prophet wrote down to pass on to others. John's prophecy was largely the second type: a report of visionary revelation, but it also included elements of oracular prophecy, most notable being

33 Marva J. Dawn, *Joy in Our Weakness: A Gift of Hope from the Book of Revelation*, rev. ed. (Grand Rapids, MI: Wm. B. Eerdmans Publishing Co., 2002).

the prologue (1:8), the epilogue (22:12-13) and the messages to the seven churches (2:1-3:22). Bauckham further clarified the nature of John's prophecy:

> Yet if Revelation resembles in a very general way the kind of prophecy John might have delivered orally in person, it is also a far more elaborate and studied composition than any extemporary prophecy could have been. Revelation is a literary work composed with astonishing care and skill. We should certainly not doubt that John had remarkable visionary experiences, but he has transmuted them through what must have been a lengthy process of reflection and writing into a thoroughly literary creation which is designed not to reproduce the experience so much as to communicate the meaning of the revelation that had been given him. Certainly Revelation is a literary work designed for oral performance (1:3), but as a complex literary creation, dense with meaning and allusion, it must be qualitatively different from the spontaneous orality of most early Christian prophecy.[34]

Originally, John's prophecy may have been based on the visionary experiences he had, but these have been transformed through extensive reflection, perhaps over years of ministry, into a literary creation. This is crucial for understanding Revelation because it refutes the popular notion that John was simply taking dictation while receiving a vision, and that the real author is Jesus. Such a literal understanding of inspiration is far too simplistic and does not sufficiently take into consideration the obvious literary characteristics of Revelation.

Consider, for example, John's extensive use of contemporary sources. John draws on Greek and Roman myths, parodies Roman political formulas and alludes to non-canonical Jewish writings. One of the truly astounding characteristics of John's preaching is his use of Hebrew scripture. While no direct quotations are

34 Bauckham, *The Theology of the Book of Revelation*, 3-4.

made, there are over 600 allusions to Old Testament passages:

> It seems that John not only writes in the tradition
> of the Old Testament prophets, but understands
> himself to be writing at the climax of the tradition,
> when all the eschatological oracles of the prophets
> are about to be finally fulfilled, and so he interprets
> and gathers them up in his own prophetic revelation.
> What makes him a Christian prophet is that he
> does so in the light of the fulfillment already of Old
> Testament prophetic expectation in the victory of
> the lamb, the Messiah Jesus.[35]

John stands in a tradition with other New Testament authors of
appropriating scripture (Old Testament) and reinterpreting it for
a new time and new community. This technique of intertextuality
is common to Paul and the four gospel writers. Instead of direct
quotations and the use of the prophetic fulfillment formula
("this took place in order to fulfill what was spoken through the
prophet..."), John uses indirect echoes and allusions to scripture,
demonstrating his willingness not just to hand on but to reshape
the tradition in which he stands:

> Here is what we find as we consider the
> relationship of preaching to the biblical texts:
> The Bible provides the source and the criterion
> of faithful preaching. Sermons start with texts;
> however, preaching is not just a matter of reading
> the scripture in a loud voice, or dramatically. New
> occasions demand new interpretations, shifted
> nuances, applications that our forebears never
> dreamed.... Fortunately, scripture itself provides a
> multitude of examples of doing just what preachers
> have to do: take a text or tradition and reshape it or
> reapply it to the issues of a new time, or the needs
> of a different community.[36]

35 Ibid, 5.
36 Bartlett, Between the Bible and the Church: New Methods for Biblical
Preaching, 16.

In his use of scripture, John becomes a good example of what preachers of biblical texts do by translating God's word into new contexts.[37]

Continuity with Old Testament Prophetic Preaching

Revelation's claim to be prophecy must be seen within the whole biblical prophetic tradition. The word, "prophecy," is often understood by many in our modern culture as prediction of the future. This is a reductionistic misunderstanding of biblical prophecy. The Hebrew prophets brought messages of judgment and hope to God's people. When the people were unfaithful to God's covenant, the prophets called them to repent. The sins they condemned were not just religious, but they had social, economic and political consequences. For the most part, the Hebrew prophets were astute observers of the political scene and spoke God's word into specific social and political contexts. The predictive nature of prophetic speech was largely the call to avoid God's future judgment. This future was not inevitable, but contingent on the response of God's people. Those who see prophecy narrowly as the prediction of the future have a deterministic view of history, a view the prophets did not share at all.

Revelation stands solidly in this prophetic tradition. The call of Christ in the messages to the seven churches in Revelation 2-3 sounds like the Old Testament prophets in their condemnation of sin, call to repentance and words of encouragement. While there is an element of future prediction in Revelation, the new heaven and new earth at the end of the book, Revelation is first and foremost a word from God for its own time:

> Perplexed as they faced new critical situations for which their Bible and traditional teachings of Jesus gave little direct guidance, those who wanted to be faithful Christians in this new situation

37 For a complete list of Old Testament allusions see the book: *Charts on the Book of Revelation: Literary, Historical, and Theological Perspectives* by Mark Wilson. Kregel Academic & Professional, 2007.

needed a word from the Lord to direct them. They needed to understand their present situation and what Christian faithfulness required of them in it. Prophets were not predictors of historical events of the distant future but were inspired interpreters of the historical events through which their hearers were living. This is already clear from a reading of the biblical prophets.[38]

John encouraged his readers to *keep* his prophecy (Revelation 1:3). One cannot "keep" future predictions, but one can "keep" a call to repentance and faithfulness. "When interpreted responsibly, Revelation has a message *to* our time, but it does not make predictions *about* it."[39]

Significantly, the book itself defines what prophecy is: "For the testimony of Jesus is the spirit of prophecy" (Revelation 19:10). Here, prophecy is defined as the proclamation of Christ. "The criterion for authentic prophecy is finally whether the prophet's message promotes faithfulness to God or whether it leads people away from God."[40] True prophetic speech presents the claims of Christ and calls the church to faithfulness. This prophecy also exposes the idolatrous claims of the dominant culture and proclaims an alternative reality based on the promises of God to make all things new. This, in essence, is what Christian and biblical preaching is all about — the faithful proclamation of Christ so that each new generation can be reconciled to God.

Interpretive Approaches to Revelation

In his essay, "Preaching Apocalyptic? You've Got to be Kidding," Gordon Fee named the reluctance many pastors feel when it comes to preaching the book of Revelation. He urged pastors to recapture Revelation from the dispensationalists

38 M. Eugene Boring, *Revelation*, ed. James L. Mays. Interpretation, a Bible Commentary for Teaching and Preaching (Louisville, KY: John Knox Press, 1989), 25.
39 Ibid, 24.
40 Craig R. Koester, *Revelation and the End of All Things* (Grand Rapids, MI: Wm. B. Eerdmans Publishing Co., 2001), 45.

and proclaim its hopeful message to the church today. In order to preach Revelation well, Fee argued, one needs to first learn how to read it well. The basic hermeneutical question is, "How is the preacher to interpret Revelation?" The interpretive glasses preachers wear will greatly influence what they see in Revelation's pages. Those who want to preach Revelation must be clear about the presuppositions they bring to the text. They also need to be ready to explain those presuppositions to their congregations. "Hearers will notice if we change our hermeneutical or homiletical methods in dealing with apocalyptic texts. As responsible leaders of the church, preachers must stand willing to explain both how they employ biblical texts and why."[41]

Throughout history, interpretations of Revelation have tended to fall into one of four major schools. They are: the preterist school, the historicist school, the futurist school, and the symbolic school.[42]

The word "preterist" means "past." This school of thought locates the meaning of Revelation in the past, in the specific historical context for which it was written. It denies that Revelation has any meaning or significance for the future. It also has no relevance for today, other than as an historical document for study. This attitude is that of the historian studying any ancient document seeking to reconstruct the past. There may be lessons to be learned from studying Revelation, but there are no lessons intended by the author.

The historicist school understands Revelation to be a timeline of western history. This interpreter views the chapters of Revelation as a prediction of specific historic events. If one can interpret correctly, one should be able to pinpoint the current location on the timeline, and also to know when exactly the world is going to end. This school has many similarities with the futurist school.

The school of thought most familiar to the general populace is the futurist school. A futurist interpretation believes that the bulk

41 Larry Paul Jones and Jerry L. Sumney, *Preaching Apocalyptic Texts* (St. Louis, MO: Chalice Press, 1999), 4.
42 Farmer, *Revelation*, 3.

of Revelation's message was written to describe events at the end of history when Christ returns. Much like the historicist approach, the futurist interpretation views chapters 2-3 as an outline of church history. However, it departs from the historicist approach by interpreting the rest of Revelation's message in chapters 4-20 as future, describing events of a seven-year tribulation that end with a cosmic battle and the return of Christ.

The fourth major school of thought is the symbolic school, that asserts that Revelation has no ties to history at all, past, present or future. Revelation, it suggests, does not describe events in the past or predict events in the future. Rather, Revelation sets forth timeless truths in vivid symbols and pictorial language. For example, the beast does not represent the violent oppression of the Roman Empire in first-century Asia Minor, nor does it represent an end time, antichrist figure. The beast is a symbol for tyranny, wherever and whenever it exists. By interpreting Revelation as a source of timeless spiritual truths concerning the struggle between good and evil, readers in a multitude of historical and social contexts can appropriate its meaning.

In light of these four basic interpretive approaches to Revelation, the preacher must make some critical judgments. Most scholars today consider the historicist and futurist approaches as problematic and incorrect. Many reasons exist for this assessment. First, the obsession with knowing the future may be part of human nature, but it is neither biblical nor Christian. In Acts 1:6-8, Jesus responded quite specifically when asked about the future, that it was not for his followers "to know the times or seasons that the Father has set by his own authority." Those who engage in a futurist speculation employ a hermeneutic that Saint Augustine (354-430) denounced as *fantastica fornicatio*," or mental masturbation.[43] The desire to know the details of the future is more tempting, or more fantastic, than a simple blind trust in the God who holds the future.

Another problem with the futurist approach is its

43 John H. Armstrong, "Why Some Christians Still Love Conspiracy Theories," Act3Online http://www.act3online.com/ArticlesDetail.asp?id=267 (accessed January 15, 2008).

misunderstanding of biblical prophecy. Most people today think of prophecy as predicting the future, in the way that Nostradamus (1503-1566) was said to make predictions of the distant future. Although some predictive elements are to be found in the Bible, this view of prophecy is not the primary biblical understanding. As noted above, prophets were preachers who spoke God's message to the people of their own generation. Their task was not to foretell the future, but to *forthtell* or proclaim God's word to the present. Prophets were interpreters of history, bringing God's perspective on the events of their day. The author of Revelation stands firmly in this tradition, interpreting the situation of his congregation from God's perspective.

A third difficulty with the futurist school is its deterministic view of history. It understands the future as things that *must* happen. However, the biblical prophets, when they did predict the future, did so to show the outcome of the present course of action in which the people were engaged. The prophets called for repentance in order to avoid terrible future consequences. What they predicted was never an inevitable timetable of events. The God they preached was not vengeful or vindictive, but one who cared for people and desired their salvation. The prophet Jonah is a good example. The judgment Jonah predicted for Ninevah was averted because the Ninevites repented. Much to Jonah's disappointment, God demonstrated mercy when Jonah would have preferred that God show vengeance.

Finally, a futurist understanding of Revelation makes the audacious assumption that most of the book would have had no meaning for its original first-century readers. How would knowing the events that would not occur for two thousand years offer any hope or encouragement in their situation? For these reasons, a futurist interpretation is deemed inadequate and inappropriate.

Most scholars today approach the book of Revelation with some combination of the preterist and the symbolic schools of thought. An appropriate reading of Revelation begins by understanding the book's original first-century context. John was writing to real people about real concerns. What would the symbols in Revelation have meant to them? To the extent that the original meaning can be determined, preachers then have a guide that can help in evaluating future interpretations of those symbols. In his commentary on Revelation, Ron Farmer explains this approach to interpreting the text:

> I read Revelation in much the same way that I read Romans: with a view both to the original readers' situation and to my contemporary setting.... I am convinced that what a biblical text might come to mean in a new setting can be far more important than anything it has meant to past readers.[44]

An historical understanding may constrain our interpretation of Revelation, so that the interpreter cannot make Revelation say anything he or she wants it to say, but an historical understanding will not limit our interpretation of Revelation's symbols as they continue to speak with power, guided by the Holy Spirit, in ever new situations.

Two further hermeneutical considerations are important. One is that Revelation is better interpreted as a whole entity, as a complete narrative with its own integrity. Individual symbols need to be read and interpreted within the context of the whole story:

> To preach Revelation is not simply to preach a piece of it. Preaching the whole book is really an attempt to reconstruct for the contemporary audience the world that the text creates. An approach to the whole might summarize each section and then bring the vision together.... When one experiences the book as a whole it becomes not so much a sequence of events — in code — that need to be figured out. Rather the visions are variations on a theme.... Beneath it all lies the same tune, the song of triumph of God and the lamb,

44 Farmer, *Revelation*, 8.

the vindication of the saints and the final defeat of evil.[45]

Those who approach Revelation from a futurist hermeneutic often impose upon it a "metanarrative of apocalyptic dogma"[46] that borrows scriptural passages from various parts of the Bible to be assembled like pieces of a puzzle. To take Revelation as a whole means reading it from beginning to end, instead of selecting various parts of the Bible in support of an argument foreign to its basic message. We cannot interpret the parts of Revelation in ways that are incompatible with its overarching theology.

Secondly, interpreters need to remember that the book of Revelation itself is part of a larger whole, the canon of scripture. For preachers, that larger context will give some guidance in interpreting Revelation. After all, the book of Revelation is the church's book, and the church should have some say in constraining its meaning. Preachers interpret Scripture as members of a community of shared presuppositions and theological convictions. This author reads Revelation through the lens of a Lutheran theology of the cross. The book of Revelation is first and foremost a revelation of Jesus Christ (Revelation 1:1). The dominant image for Christ in Revelation is the lamb that was slaughtered. It is through this hermeneutical center that all its parts are interpreted.

An Apocalypse, a Prophecy, and a Letter

Many commentators insist that contemporary preachers can avoid hermeneutical errors by taking seriously what Revelation says about itself. One of the basic questions to ask of Revelation is, "What kind of literature is it?" When people read a text, they bring certain assumptions that impact how they read it. People would not read Tolkien's novels, *The Lord of the Rings*, the same way they would read Al Gore's book, *An Inconvenient Truth*. Those who approach Revelation as "history written in advance" will read it with a certain set of expectations.

45 Philip A. Quanbeck II, "Preaching Apocalyptic Texts," *Word & World* 25.3 (2005): 323-4.
46 Ibid, 319.

In the first few verses of the book, Revelation identifies itself as three different types of literature: apocalypse, prophecy, and letter. When interpreting the book of Revelation, preachers must keep these different genres firmly in mind.

The first word in the Greek text of Revelation is *apokalypsis*, and literally means "to unveil or remove the covering." It contains the sense of discovery, of making a revelation. What is being revealed is the risen and glorified Christ. Unfortunately, what is being revealed is often obscured by the title given the book in many Bibles today, the Revelation to John. The revelation is not primarily about the future; it is about Jesus Christ.

John's apocalypse stood squarely in a long and well-known tradition of apocalypses. The book of Daniel is one canonical example that has many characteristics of an apocalypse. The Apocalypse Group of the Society of Biblical Literature Genres Project developed a definition of apocalypse in 1986:

> Apocalypse is a genre of revelatory literature with a narrative framework, in which a revelation is mediated by an otherworldly being to a human recipient, disclosing a transcendent reality which is both temporal, insofar as it envisages eschatological salvation, and spatial insofar as it involves another, supernatural world intended to interpret present, earthly circumstances in light of the supernatural world and of the future, and to influence both the understanding and the behavior of the audience by means of divine authority.[47]

Knowing something about apocalyptic literature in general can help readers know how to interpret the book of Revelation. Modern readers, unfamiliar with apocalyptic literature, are often intrigued by Revelation because of its unique content in the Bible. The original readers, however, would have understood Revelation as an apocalypse, an established literary form, and interpreted it accordingly. Because they were familiar with this

47 David Schnasa Jacobsen, *Preaching in the New Creation: The Promise of New Testament Apocalyptic Texts* (Louisville, KY: Westminster John Knox Press, 1999), 6.

genre and its stock use of symbols and language, they would have understood how to more accurately interpret John's apocalypse. Modern interpreters do well to pay attention to the characteristics of apocalyptic literature and let that guide them in their interpretation of Revelation.

The second word John used to describe his book is "prophecy." As stated earlier, prophets spoke primarily to their time. They engaged in future prediction only to warn people of the consequences of their actions. The word, "prophecy," is important to John in describing his work. Understood in its biblical context, the designation as prophecy can aid in contemporary interpretation.

Even though John's writing is usually referred to as the "book" of Revelation, it was in reality a letter. Much like letters today, ancient letters had certain standard elements. The opening included an identification of the sender and the recipients, and an extended greeting. Like Paul's letters, Revelation contains these elements, both at the beginning and the conclusion. Also, like Paul's letters, the author and recipients are real persons in the context of a particular pastoral concern. The letter was intended to be read aloud in the worship services of those churches to address the needs of the community:

> The fact that Revelation is a letter has important consequences for understanding it. It is the nature of a letter to have a particular address. As a letter, Revelation was not written to the public at large. It was not even a general circular letter, addressing typical situations in first-century Christianity; it was written to specific Christians in a specific place, time, and situation. And it was *not* written to *us*. Just as the first letter of Paul to the Corinthians was not written to us, so the letter of John to the seven churches of Asia was not written to us. Just as we will certainly misunderstand Paul if we ignore the particularities of the situation in first-century Corinth, so we will misunderstand Revelation if we

read it as though it were written directly to us. If we want to understand Revelation, the first principle is to read it in terms of its original hearer-readers and their situation.[48]

Preachers today do well to remember that Revelation was a letter, written in a particular time to a particular people, and to approach the interpretation of Revelation in the same manner they seek to interpret the other letters of the New Testament.

The book of Revelation does present unique challenges to the contemporary reader or preacher. It is to these challenges that the author now turns.

---

48 Boring, *Revelation*, 7.

Responding To Objections To Preaching Revelation

"You Must Prophesy Again About Many Peoples And Nations"

Chapter one identified a number of reasons why many mainline preachers avoid preaching from the book of Revelation today. Some of the reasons are internal to the text, others are external. The first half of this chapter responds to eight major internal objections by bringing to bear the helpful work of several leading biblical scholars who have thought deeply and critically about the book of Revelation. The second half of this chapter will deal with what we have called external objections, or problems that discourage preachers from preaching Revelation. Some constructive proposals are offered to help preachers educate congregations about Revelation's message and rehabilitate Revelation as a rich resource for preaching and worship.

Addressing Internal Reasons Preachers Avoid the Book of Revelation

Many contemporary commentators make helpful suggestions for proclaiming Revelation's message in theologically responsible ways. Two, in particular, deserve special mention. M. Eugene Boring's commentary, *Revelation,* is part of the series, *Interpretation: A Bible Commentary for Teaching and Preaching.* The second is Ron Farmer's commentary, *Revelation,* part of the series, *Chalice Commentaries for Today.* Both series seek to provide pastors with resources to aid in teaching and preaching. This chapter draws heavily upon their work and others, in an effort to dispel or discredit many of the reservations preachers express about Revelation.

How Soon is Soon? The Expectation of an Imminent End

In the opening and closing words of Revelation, John gave voice to the expectation that Jesus would return very soon (Revelation 1:1, 3; 22:10, 12, 20). This imminent eschatology was an expectation John shared with many other New Testament authors. Some evidence exists of a growing crisis in the early church over the Lord's delayed return, and the need to reinterpret that expectation (2 Peter 3:1-10). Two thousand years later, does this expectation need to be rejected as simply wrong, or does it need to be reinterpreted:

> When John said "the time is near" (1:3), he meant the time for the happening of all the events his letter envisions, including the return of Christ, the destruction of evil, and the everlasting glory of the new world…. Does this mean he was wrong? Yes. Christians who reverence the Bible as scripture, the vehicle of God's word, ought not to hesitate to acknowledge that its authors made errors. It is an aspect of the humanity of the Bible, a part of the meaning of the incarnation, that God uses human thought (with its errors) and human beings (with their errors) to communicate his message…. Just as John accepted a flat earth with corners as the spatial framework within which he expressed his message (cf. 7:1), so he accepted a world shortly to come to an end as its temporal framework. As he was wrong in the one case, so was he wrong in the other case. But in neither case does the error of his worldview nullify the validity of the message expressed…. There is nonetheless something for the modern reader to receive from the early church's expectation of the near end of history: Without sharing their chronology, we can share their sense of urgency, the sense that our generation is the only

generation we have in which to fulfill our calling.[49]

In the early church's sense of urgency, preachers will recognize the traditional themes of the season of Advent. The time to respond to God's grace is always "now," for none knows the hour of Christ's return.

The Nature of Power in Revelation

The book of Revelation presents two quite different and contrasting views of power: the suffering, non-violent redemptive power of the lamb in chapter 5, and the coercive, violent power of the beast in chapter 13. These contrasting views of power hold great promise for preaching a relevant word to congregations today.

Many scholars believe that Revelation 5 is the interpretive key to the whole book. In this chapter, John sees a scroll in the right hand of the one seated on the throne. This scroll "contains the secret purpose of God for establishing his kingdom."[50] No one is found worthy to open the scroll and accomplish God's purposes. John next hears and sees something. "The key to John's vision of the slaughtered lamb (5:6) is to recognize the contrast between what he hears (5:5) and what he sees (5:6)."[51] John hears, "the lion of the tribe of Judah, the root of David who has conquered." The language used to describe the lion, borrowed from several Old Testament passages, meets the common expectations for a strong militaristic leader. This is what John hears; what John sees, however, is completely different. John sees "a lamb standing as if it had been slaughtered." The two images are dialectical opposites. They reinterpret and explain each other. The reader has no doubt that the slain lamb now standing refers to Jesus' death and resurrection. Moreover, John describes the lamb with seven horns and seven eyes, symbols used to portray perfect power and perfect wisdom. By juxtaposing these two opposing images, John is making a profound theological statement: the

49 Ibid, 72-3.
50 Bauckham, *The Theology of the Book of Revelation*, 74.
51 Ibid

most powerful force in the universe, the only force worthy and able to accomplish God's purposes, is the suffering redemptive love demonstrated in the death of Christ. This power of Christ crucified is foolishness to the world, "but to those who are the called, both Jews and Greeks, Christ the power of God and the wisdom of God" (1 Corinthians 1:24). True power is here being redefined by John, not as brute force, but as suffering, redemptive love. "The paradox resulting from the dialectical relationship between what John hears (militant lion) and what he sees (slaughtered lamb) powerfully proclaims that *God's victory, God's conquest, is achieved only through redemptive love, a love willing to suffer if need be.*"[52]

This redefinition of power as suffering redemptive love compels us to think deeply about our views of God and how God still influences the world:

> First, God's power is presented as *persuasive* and *all-influencing* rather than coercive and all-controlling. God does influence every creature, seeking to lure or persuade it toward the optimum mode for its development. Still, each creature remains genuinely free to choose the degree to which it will follow the divine will. Second, power is *relational* rather than unilateral, that is, power flows in all directions. Because reality is thoroughly interrelated, everything affects everything else. Not only does God influence every creature, but every creaturely event also affects God. God feels every earthly joy and sorrow.[53]

The lamb imagery subverts every notion of God as controlling all that happens, or of a God who is apathetic or unchanging in response to the suffering of the creation.

The lion/lamb dialectic not only leads us to rethink our images of God, but also to reevaluate how God's purposes are carried out in the church:

52 Farmer, *Revelation*, 64.
53 Ibid, 66.

Jesus' sacrificial death may have enabled God to *inaugurate* the divine purpose, but the *continued* implementation of God's purpose depends on the followers of Jesus making his lifestyle their lifestyle. Obviously, heeding John's exhortation requires a radically new understanding of reality, one in which a slaughtered lamb conquers and faithful testimony — accompanied by voluntary, redemptive suffering, even to the point of martyrdom if need be — results in the overthrow of evil and the establishment of God's purposes for creation.[54]

In the book of Revelation, the symbol of this lion/lamb is one of the major interpretive lenses for understanding not only Revelation, but for understanding reality itself.

Richard Bauckham makes a similar point, arguing that the mission of the lamb gives shape to the mission of the church. The unfolding judgments in the series of seals and trumpets in chapters 6-9 are not enough to bring about the conversion of the nations (6:16; 9:20). Not until hearing and seeing the example of the two witnesses do the nations come to repentance (Revelation 11:13):

> To be the witnesses who bring the nations to faith in the one true God is the novel role of God's eschatological people, revealed by the scroll that only the lamb has been able to open. If we ask how the prophetic witness of the church is able to have this effect, which that of the Old Testament prophets did not, the answer is no doubt that it derives its power from the victory of the lamb himself. His witness had the power of a witness maintained even to the point of death and then vindicated as true witness by his resurrection. The witness of his followers participates in this power when they too are faithful witnesses even to death.... In fact,

54 Ibid, 67.

the way that Christian martyrdom, in the early centuries of the church, impressed and won people to faith in the Christian God, was precisely thus. The martyrs were effective witnesses to the truth of the gospel because their faith in Christ's victory over death was so convincingly evident in the way they faced death and died.[55]

When seen in this way, John's call to the church is a call to conquer through its non-violent witness and participation in Christ's suffering and redemptive love. In Revelation, the power of love changes people and leads them to Christ.

Revelation contrasts the power of the lamb with the power of the beast. The beast exercises control through violence and coercion. The inhabitants of the earth, who worship the beast, ask in 13:4, "Who is like the beast, and who can fight against it?" The answer is given in 12:11, "But they have conquered him by the blood of the lamb and by the word of their testimony, for they did not cling to life even in the face of death." Brought face to face with the fearful power of the beast God's people cling in hope to a greater power:

> Revelation's first-century readers knew firsthand Rome's conquering power over the whole world. They were its victims. We, too, live in a world in which terror makes us feel powerless and we wonder how God can be victorious over evil. The "beasts" of violence, economic vulnerability, global injustice and other threats still stalk our world, causing almost irrational fear. In a post-September 11 world, we need to testify to the wonder-working power of God's slain lamb today more than ever. Revelation's message is that the beasts and their conquering do not have the last word.[56]

Rather than representing a different Jesus not found in the gospels, Revelation stands in continuity with the non-violent

55 Bauckham, *The Theology of the Book of Revelation*, 87-8.
56 Rossing, *The Rapture Exposed: The Message of Hope in the Book of Revelation*, 120.

teaching of Jesus in the Sermon on the Mount. The church is called to turn the other cheek, to love its enemies, to come out of Babylon (Revelation 18:4) and forsake its idolatrous worship of wealth and power. In a world addicted to violence, this message is powerful and relevant for the church today.

The Violent Imagery of Revelation

When people read Revelation, they are often repulsed by its violent images and horrors. How are contemporary preachers to deal with this? M. Eugene Boring offers four helpful observations, paraphrased below, that can help preachers come to terms with Revelation's violent world.[57]

First, John was giving voice to the experience of suffering that was endured by some of the Christian communities to whom he was writing. When people suffer, they typically experience feelings of resentment or vengeance. Those who have not experienced such suffering may have a hard time understanding that the cries for vengeance in Revelation (Revelation 6:9-11) are, in reality, cries for justice. This reframing of the motivation allows the text to speak fruitfully instead of fiercely.

Second, much of the violence in Revelation was appropriated by John from his sources. Many of the Old Testament passages that John alludes to contain violent language and imagery. John borrows extensively from the violent Exodus story, using it as a kind of template. John also makes use of a widely known ancient Near Eastern combat myth of creation.

Third, John uses language in metaphorical or symbolic ways. The sword coming from Jesus' mouth by which he conquers is not a literal sword, but rather a metaphor for the power of God's word to cut to the heart, to distinguish and separate good from evil. One must bear in mind that John intended these images to be heard in the context of worship. This is confessional language by which John communicates God's care for the worshipper. It does not mean that God is unconcerned about others. Those outside the worshipping community may hear this language as judgmental. For example, at the end of the series of seal devastations, the

57 Boring, *Revelation*, 112-9.

people of the earth interpret their sufferings, "Fall on us and hide us from the face of the one seated on the throne and from the wrath of the lamb" (Revelation 6:16). It is common for human beings to attribute negative events to the anger of God. Every pastor has dealt with that. The responsibility of the followers of the lamb is to offer a better interpretation of those events and give witness to the true nature of the lamb.

Fourth, John uses violent imagery to reveal the extent of human sinfulness. In Exodus, the plagues revealed Pharaoh's hard-heartedness. People who suffer the consequences of their sin can and often do refuse to repent. What is needed is Christ's soul-piercing sword to reveal their sin and bring them to repentance.

The language of violence that John used is transformed by his primary Christological symbol, the presence of the lamb. "The imagery of the lion is still used, but the Messiah is the slain lamb. As in mathematics when one changes the valence of the sign outside the parentheses, the formulae within the parentheses are retained, but all their values are reversed."[58] The violent images in Revelation are given new meaning by the presence of the lamb.

Preachers will be tempted to quickly interpret or explain away the disturbing images of violence in Revelation. David Barr gives a final caution:

> Viewed at the level of symbolism, the apocalypse indulges in images of great violence and oppression.... Careful reading will show that John always subverts these images, but the apocalypse is not always carefully read. And we must ask, even if we read John's images carefully, can we ever overcome their sheer brutality? Can any amount of hermeneutical legerdemain ever hide the naked, brutalized, cannibalized woman whom John uses as the symbol for imperial evil? Such images remain morally deficient whatever interpretation we attach to them.[59]

58 Ibid, 118.
59 David L. Barr, "The lamb Who Looks Like a Dragon? Characterizing Jesus in John's Apocalypse," *In The Reality of Apocalypse: Rhetoric and Politics in the Book of Revelation*, ed. David L. Barr, Symposium (Atlanta, GA: Society of Biblical Literature, 2006), 210.

Understanding God's Anger and the Wrath of the Lamb

Though out of fashion, the most common characterization of Revelation preaching today is the "fire and brimstone" variety, designed literally, "to scare the hell out of people." The threat of punishment is meant to move humans to repent and behave. Many people are familiar with Old Testament passages that portray a God who directly punishes people for their sins. The language of Revelation can certainly be seen in this light and presents a challenge for modern interpreters. For example, when God's enemies are tormented "with fire and sulphur in the presence of the holy angels and in the presence of the lamb" (14:10) modern people are troubled by the seeming malice and vindictiveness:

> That such a fiery torture can be envisioned is horrible; that the lamb can be envisioned as a spectator to it is beyond horror. And it gets worse, for one must raise here the specter of coercion. Humanity seems left in the impossible situation that the beast will kill all those who do not worship it (13:15) and God will kill and torture all those who do (14:9-11). It seems a fine line between killing to induce worship and killing because of worship.... The degree of violence, involving eternal torture, and the participation of the lamb, at least as spectator, raises acutely the question of how John intends to characterize Jesus.[60]

A closer reading of the text is required to understand John's use of symbols. Throughout Revelation John reinterprets traditional images of divine anger and judgment:

> Again we find a radical symbolic inversion: images of power are replaced by images of suffering. Similar inversions occur at every point in the story — even in the climactic scene in which the heavenly warrior kills all his enemies, for his conquest is by means of a sword that comes from his mouth, not

60 Ibid, 207-8.

by the power of his arm (19:21). Thus the victory over evil is procured not by physical violence but by verbal power. Surely this story is built on the mythology of holy war (and that itself may be ethically problematic), but just as surely John consistently demythologizes the war — or perhaps more accurately, remythologizes the warrior with the image of the suffering Savior so that the death of the warrior and not some later battle is the crucial event. At every juncture in this story where good triumphs over evil a close examination shows that the victory is finally attributed to the death of Jesus.[61]

To find in Revelation a malicious and punitive God is to engage in too shallow a reading of the text.

Rather than attributing violence to divine retribution, Revelation points us in another direction:

> Thus in the scene of the destruction of the whore of Babylon …it is human brutality that is portrayed. The ten kings and the beast destroy her. Even so, this is because "God has put it into their hearts to carry out God's purpose" (17:17). Thus in some way God must be held accountable for all the violence in the world, even human violence, for God is responsible for creation. But this is surely morally different than imagining divine violence. In fact, John signals this dialectical tension by immediately adding, "The woman you saw is the great city that rules over the kings of the earth" (17:18). Those who seek to dominate others will themselves be devoured by the process; it is, John says, what God has ordained. While the image of violence is problematic …the understanding of violence is not.[62]

61 David L Barr, "Doing Violence: Moral Issues in Reading John's Apocalypse," In *Reading the Book of Revelation: A Resource for Students*, ed. David L. Barr (Atlanta, GA: Society of Biblical Literature, 2003), 101.
62 Barr, *The Lamb Who Looks Like a Dragon? Characterizing Jesus in John's Apocalypse*. 214-5.

Sin has a self-defeating character. Rather than the result of divine action, the violence portrayed in Revelation is often best understood as the consequence of the destructiveness inherent in any system that relies on domination.

Hints of another perspective on divine anger and judgment can be observed in scripture:

> This is not, however, the Bible's only (or most mature) understanding of divine wrath. For example, in his letter to the Romans, the apostle Paul described divine wrath as God's "giving people up" (1:18, 24, 26, 28) to experience the consequences of their sinful actions, in hope that the undesirable consequences of sin would serve as a call to repentance. God redemptively transforms the evil caused by human sin into a call to repentance.[63]

Suffering may not be a direct punishment inflicted by God, but rather the consequence of sin. God can use suffering as a warning that something is wrong, and call people to repentance.

The depiction of a wrathful God is not unique to Revelation. What is unique is the way it is presented. While the apostle Paul can rationally argue that "the wages of sin is death" (Romans 6:23), John will take the reader into the frightening apocalyptic world of demonic locusts, earthquakes and pestilence. Both are communicating the same message, but by different means:

> By using extreme images to depict God's response to evil, John forces us to come to terms with the magnitude of the problem of sin. It is not some minor issue that can be resolved by a simple, painless solution. On the contrary, it is a matter of crucial importance that requires drastic measures to resolve. Though we understand the reasons why Revelation presents the wrath of God as it does, this must not diminish the horror or the fear that the book provokes. We are supposed to feel terror and revulsion at its scenes of destruction and carnage,

63 Farmer, *Revelation*, 82.

not so that we will cringe pathetically before God like frightened and ill-treated dogs, but so that we will actually feel some of the drama that the book is trying to communicate and take our stance of faith accordingly. Revelation does not speak to us simply on the level of our minds. It speaks to our emotions as well.[64]

The emotional impact Revelation intends will point us beyond an angry vindictive God, to a loving God who will go to extreme measures to free God's creation from its bondage to sin.

The Nature of Evil in Revelation

The book of Revelation is in harmony with much of early Christianity in using the language and symbol of Satan to explain the presence of evil in the world. John portrayed in cosmic terms the battle first-century Christians experienced on earth. The real enemy was not "flesh and blood," but the power of evil, symbolized by the dragon. The dragon was defeated in heaven and thrown down to earth for a short while to wage war on the saints before its ultimate destruction. John's unique contribution to this mythological symbology is in portraying evil embodied in the Roman imperial system. The beast represents Roman military conquest and the coercive threat of violence to ensure allegiance. The whore represents the seductive power of the Roman economy and the promise of wealth and luxury to motivate faithfulness to Rome. What is being "revealed" by John (Revelation 1:1) is the very nature of evil institutionalized in the Roman Empire. "All these 'super-personal forces of evil' are not speculative abstractions for John and his church, but are met in their embodiments in the social structures of John's situation and in the institutionalized evil of the Roman Empire."[65] What John did in Revelation was to reveal to the Christians in Asia Minor their real enemy. John identified Satan as the "accuser of our comrades" (12:10), a powerful designation for those Christians

---

64 Paul Spilsbury, *The Throne, the Lamb & the Dragon: A Reader's Guide to the Book of Revelation* (Downers Grove, IL: InterVarsity Press, 2002), 128.
65 Boring, *Revelation*, 166.

who found themselves accused in Roman courts. For those Christians who prospered from participating in the economy, John identified Satan as the "great whore," the seducer who numbed their spirits into the worship of the false gods of worldly success.

How are contemporary preachers to make use of this language? When speaking of the evils in our world today, many share the conviction that evil is more than just the sum total of individual human sins:

> Many contemporary Christian theologians with a deep social conscience have found the New Testament's imagery for the demonic power of evil to be valuable when taken seriously, but not literally. "Satan" as a symbolic way of thinking of the super-personal power of evil is a valuable dimension of biblical theology. The power of evil is bigger than individual sins. John consistently speaks in terms of political and national terms when he talks of the power of Satan (13:7; 18:3, 23; 20:3, 8). Satan is not merely the individualistic tempter to petty sins; he is the deceiver of the nations (20:7-8). We might now label this as "systemic evil," or picture it more in accord with our own times as a vast impersonal computer-like network of evil in which our lives are enmeshed and which influences us quite apart from our wills.[66]

When interpreted in this way, the language and symbol of Satan can provide a profound theological truth that speaks to our times.

One theologian who has translated the language of Satan into twenty-first- century terms is Walter Wink. In his book, *The Powers That Be: Theology for a New Millennium*, Wink describes the "powers that be" as those spiritual forces that inhabit every institution and system that impinge on and determine our lives. Wink bases his work on the Pauline concept of the principalities

66 Ibid, 167.

and powers (Ephesians 6:12; Romans 8:38). He also draws from other parts of scripture, notably the letters to the angels of the seven churches in Rev 2-3. The letters are not addressed to the congregation, but to the congregations' angel, the corporate climate, personality or spirit of the church. In other parts of the Bible, cities and nations also have angels (Daniel 10). Wink understands this to mean that everything has an inner and outer aspect, a spiritual and physical dimension.

> The powers that be are not, then, simply people and their institutions, as I had first thought; they also include the spirituality at the core of those institutions and structures…. The spirituality that we encounter in institutions is not always benign. It is just as likely to be pathological. And this is where the biblical understanding of the powers surpasses in profundity the best of modern sociology. For the angel of an institution is not just the sum total of all that an institution is (which sociology is competent to describe); it is also the bearer of that institution's divine vocation (which sociology is not able to discern). Corporations and governments are "creatures" whose sole purpose is to serve the general welfare. And when they refuse to do so, their spirituality becomes diseased. They become "demonic."

> I had never been able to take demons seriously. The idea that fallen angels possessed people seemed superstitious. But if the demonic is the spirituality produced when the angel of an institution turns its back on its divine vocation, then I could not only believe in the demonic, I could point to its presence in everyday life. And if the demonic arises when an angel deviates from its calling, then social change does not depend on casting out the demon but recalling its angel to its divine task.[67]

67 Walter Wink, *The Powers That Be: Theology for a New Millennium* (New York: Doubleday, 1998), 4-6.

This understanding of the demonic is a useful one for preachers today, quite apart from how one answers the metaphysical questions about Satan or demons.

Wink suggests a further way for twenty-first century people to understand the biblical language about Satan:

> We might think of "demons" as the actual spirituality of systems and structures that have betrayed their divine vocations. When an entire network of powers becomes integrated around idolatrous values, we get what can be called *the Domination System....* From this perspective, "Satan" is the world-encompassing spirit of the Domination System. Do these entities possess actual metaphysical being, or are they the "corporate personality" or ethos of an institution or epoch, having no independent existence apart from their incarnation in a system? That is for the reader to decide.[68]

For Wink, the important task of the church is to identify or discern the spirits. When a particular power or institution becomes idolatrous and makes its own interests the highest good, then it becomes demonic. The church is to unmask this idolatry and recall the powers to the purposes for which God created them.

Revelation's Portrayal of Women

Some modern readers of Revelation are offended by John's negative portrayal of women that reflects values typical of the patriarchal culture of the first-century world. The book seems to convey images of women either positively as brides or negatively as whores. In her commentary, *Revelation: Vision of a Just World*, Elizabeth Schüssler Fiorenza suggests a reading strategy that focuses less on John's androcentric language and more on actual practice of reading. She asserts that, "throughout the centuries women have read and identified with great literature not because they were totally self-alienated, but because they read it as

68 Ibid, 27.

'common literature' with whose humanist values and visions they could identify."[69] This is a helpful strategy for reading Revelation today.

Schüssler Fiorenza argues that masculine or feminine language and imagery should be interpreted as generic language, unless a careful reading indicates that it functions as gender-specific language that self-consciously intends to convey patriarchal values. "Whoring and fornication as metaphors for idolatry, as well as the symbolic understanding of Israel as bride and wife of Yahweh, are part and parcel of the prophetic-apocalyptic tradition. They must be subjected to a feminist critique, but their gendered meaning cannot be assumed as primary within the narrative contextualization of Revelation."[70] For example, the army of the lamb in Rev 14:4 are those "who have not defiled themselves with women, for they are virgins." In his commentary, Boring argues that these are persons engaged in special service to God, and during the time of their service were "expected to refrain from sex, not from moralistic reasons, but to insulate the sacred service from other powers."[71] This kind of reading can assist preachers in translating the text in more gender-neutral ways that allow modern people to hear its deeper message.

Revelation and the Extent of Salvation

Jokes about someone who dies and appears before the pearly gates wanting to get into heaven are common. However, in Revelation's vision of the New Jerusalem, those gates are never shut. They stand wide open ready to receive "the glory and honor of the nations" (Revelation 21:25-6). Everyone seems to be welcomed and included. Jokes that take place in hell with people in some form of torment are also common. One of the difficult problems in interpreting Revelation is that the book portrays "two distinct and irreconcilable notions of salvation."[72] One

69 Elisabeth Schüssler Fiorenza, *Revelation: Vision of a Just World*. Proclamation Commentaries (Minneapolis, MN: Fortress Press, 1991), 14.
70 Ibid
71 Boring, *Revelation*, 169.
72 Farmer, *Revelation*, 126.

set of passages demonstrate salvation limited to certain people (Revelation 14:9-11, 14-20; 20:11-15; 21:8, 27; 22:15). Another set of texts imply a more universal salvation (Revelation 1:7; 4:3; 5:13; 15:4; 21:22-22:3).

Historically, interpreters have taken one side or the other. Boring makes the claim that both are present, both are valid interpretations in Revelation, and that it is impossible to fit them both into one consistent view:

> Neither group of texts can be subordinated to the other.... Revelation intends to present pictures in which the one sovereign and gracious God is finally victorious and restores all his creation to its intended blessedness, redeeming all his creatures (pictures in which all are saved unconditionally because of God's decision to accept them). He also intends to present pictures which portray human beings as responsible for their decisions, pictures of how inexpressibly terrible it is to reject one's creator and live one's life in allegiance to false gods (pictures in which the faithful are saved and unbelievers are damned because they did not decide to accept God). By offering pictures of both unconditional/universal and conditional/limited salvation and thus affirming both poles of the dialectic, John, in accord with biblical theology in general, guards against the dangers inherent in a superficial "consistency" obtained by affirming only one side of the issue. The interpreter's task is not to seek ways to reconcile the tension in the text; the task is to find the thrust of Revelation's message precisely in this tension.[73]

For some, this task of holding both sides in tension with each other will be unsatisfying. The temptation will be to solve the problem by elevating one side over the other.

Boring cautions that several dangers for misunderstanding exist on either side of this dialectic. He maintains that the

73 Boring, *Revelation*, 228.

doctrine of universal salvation should not be held in such a way that it "relativizes the ultimate revelation-salvation event of Jesus Christ.... that it permits the relaxation of human responsibility.... that it minimizes God's judgment on human sin.... that it minimizes the importance of faith and the urgency of evangelism."[74] On the other hand, the doctrine of limited salvation should not be affirmed in such a way that God is portrayed as vindictive or frustrated by a rebellious creation. Limited salvation images should not be explained away as a kind of purgatory on the way to universal salvation. Nor should a doctrine of limited salvation be affirmed because of the necessity of logical coherence for one's own theological beliefs.

More recently, there have been several authors who are challenging the traditional Christian teaching about heaven and hell and the doctrine of limited salvation. In 2009, Rob Bell wrote a book called, *Love Wins: A Book About Heaven, Hell, and the Fate of Every Person Who Has Ever Lived.* He wrote the book to explain the love of God as revealed in the Jesus story.

> "A staggering number of people have been taught that a select few Christians will spend forever in a peaceful, joyous place called heaven, while the rest of humanity spends forever in torment and punishment in hell with no chance for anything better. It's been clearly communicated to many that this belief is a central truth of the Christian faith and to reject it is, in essence, to reject Jesus. This is misguided and toxic and ultimately subverts the contagious spread of Jesus' message of love, peace, forgiveness, and joy that our world desperately needs to hear. And so this book."[75]

Bell invites us on a journey that not only questions the traditional teaching of hell and limited salvation, but also claims that the biblical witness is more faithfully interpreted by a more universal understanding of the love of God.

74 Ibid, 229.
75 Rob Bell, *Love Wins: A Book About Heaven, Hell and the Fate of Every Person Who Ever Lived.* (New York: Harper Collins, 2011), viii.

Another author inviting us on a similar journey is Brian McLaren. In his book, *The Last Word and the Word After That: A Tale of Faith, Doubt, and a New Kind of Christianity*, McLaren claims that our understanding of hell reveals a lot about our understanding of God.

> On the surface, this book appears to be largely about hell.... As I see it, more significant than any doctrine of hell itself is the view of God to which one's doctrine of hell contributes.... This book is, in the end, more about our view of God than it is about our understandings of hell. What kind of God do we believe exists? What kind of life should we live in response? How does our view of God affect the way we see and treat other people? And how does the way we see and treat other people affect our view of God?... Could our view of hell... be the symptoms of a deeper set of problems — misunderstandings about God's purpose in creating the world, deep misunderstandings about what kind of person God is? Those are the questions I'm pursuing in this book."[76]

One last author who wrote passionately about reinterpreting our traditional understandings of God and hell is Sharon Baker. In her book called, *Razing Hell: Rethinking Everything You've Been Taught about God's Wrath and Judgment*, Baker invites us to reimagine an alternative to traditional teachings of hell, God's wrath, and judgment.[77] She lays out a new view of hell that she claims is a more faithful reading of scripture.

Preachers who engage the book of Revelation will want to spend some time thinking through this issue. Questions about heaven and hell will certainly arise in the minds of the

76 Brian D. McLaren, *The Last Word and the Word After That: A Tale of Faith, Doubt, and a New Kind of Christianity*. (San Francisco: Jossey-Bass, 2005), xi-xiii.
77 Sharon L. Baker, *Razing Hell: Rethinking Everything You've Been Taught About God's Wrath and Judgment*. (Louisville, Kentucky: Westminster John Knox Press, 2010).

congregation.

Revelation as World Denigrating

For many people, mention of Revelation or the word "apocalypse" is synonymous with the end of the world. Post-modern media and culture use language borrowed from Revelation that is almost always cataclysmic in nature. The current global warming crisis and growing interest in caring for the environment make people wary of Revelation. However, as Ron Farmer points out, Revelation is not anti-earth or anti-environment. It is actually earth-friendly:

> John's apocalypse is decidedly world affirming. Chapter 4 clearly asserts that the present world, in spite of its evil aspects (symbolized by the sea), is God's good creation and therefore worthy of redemption.... Granted, John pointedly denounced various abuses of God's good creation — abuses perpetrated primarily through the misuse of political/military, economic, and religious power. Rather than concluding his apocalypse with a fiery negation of the world, John pictured instead a rebirth of the world — transformation, not destruction.[78]

Revelation may be exactly what an environmentally-conscious world needs.

How then shall we interpret the scenes of devastation to the environment in Revelation? As many scholars note, the destruction that accompanies the seals, trumpets and bowls in Revelation is patterned after the plagues of the Exodus story. The Exodus plagues function much the way Revelation's scenes of devastation do, namely, to change the death-dealing policies of the empire in order to liberate God's people and bring "healing to the nations." In Revelation 11:18, judgment is brought on those who destroy the earth. "The 'destroyers of the earth' are the powers of evil: the dragon, the beast, and the harlot of Babylon....

78 Farmer, *Revelation*, 61-2.

With their violence, oppression, and idolatrous religion they are ruining God's creation. His faithfulness to his creation requires that he destroy them in order to preserve and to deliver it from evil."[79] In spite of the visions of earthly destruction, Revelation is firmly earth-centered. The final vision of a new heaven and new earth is a vision of renewal and hope for *this* world:

> The New Jerusalem of Revelation 21-22 is a wonderfully earth-centered vision of our future, a vision of hope for this world. Contrary to the escapism and "heavenism" that dominates fundamentalist interpretations today, the storyline of Revelation emphasizes that our future dwelling will be with God on earth, in a radiant, thriving city landscape. The home of God is among people. From now on, God "will dwell with them as their God."

> The word "dwell" in Revelation is the same word as used to describe Jesus' coming to earth in the gospel of John, "the word became flesh and dwelt among us." The whole message of the Bible is that God loves the world so much that God comes to earth to dwell with us.[80]

Rather than encouraging a lack of concern for a planet soon to be destroyed at Christ's return, Revelation communicates God's love for the world and desire to "make all things new" (Revelation 21:5). Boring makes a similar argument:

> [God] does not junk the cosmos and start anew — he renews the old and brings it to fulfillment.

> The advent of the heavenly city does not abolish all human efforts to build a decent earthly civilization but fulfills them. God does not make 'all new things,' but 'all things new'…. John affirms this world and its value and thus pictures eternal

79 Bauckham, *The Theology of the Book of Revelation*, 52.
80 Rossing, *The Rapture Exposed: The Message of Hope in the Book of Revelation*, 148.

salvation as the salvation of the world and of history itself."[81]

Much recent scholarship has highlighted the global climate change crisis. Barbara Rossing has written how apocalypses and the book of Revelation can actually help to create a hopeful vision for the future of our planet.

> Apocalypses are essential to our preaching. They empower radical witness. They give us a sacramental imagination, taking us on a journey into the heart of God's vision for our world. Apocalypses pull back a curtain so people can see the world more deeply — both the beauty of creation and also the pathologies of empire, experienced as plagues against creation....

> We need such a radical transformation of our imaginations for eco-reformation today. In a time of climate injustice, greed, food insecurity, environmental racism, species extinctions, ocean acidification, and ecological trauma, the visionary world of apocalypses can renew our hope. They can help us see both the perils we face and the urgency of God's promised future, turning the world for justice and healing, "on earth as in heaven." The preacher cultivates an apocalyptic imagination by helping people recognize God's future breaking into the present, even in times of despair.

> My goal is to encourage preaching on apocalyptic scripture so people hear the urgent good news: God's kingdom is drawing near. New birth is dawning on earth. Scripture is coming to life. Healing is springing forth. The world is about to turn. And God's people participate in that apocalyptic turning, as living witnesses to the hope

81 Boring, *Revelation*, 220.

and healing eco-reformation can bring.[82]

A preacher who is serious about stewardship of the planet need not fear Revelation but can find in it a divine mandate for caring for creation.

Addressing External Reasons Preachers Avoid the Book of Revelation

While the preceding internal reasons preachers avoid Revelation are largely theological in nature, the external reasons are more practical. Many pastors have simply received no training at the seminary in preaching apocalyptic texts. With increasing interest in apocalyptic themes in our culture, many seminaries are taking steps to overcome this.

Preachers can search far and wide to find homiletical materials to help them venture into Revelation's strange territory. Most of the resources that are available for mainline preachers are geared toward the lectionary. Publishers realize this is what sells, and so that is what they provide.

It is ironic that the best-selling "Christian" books in recent years have been those of the *Left Behind* series. The mainline churches may be ignoring Revelation, but other churches are not. While pastors are suspicious of the dispensationalist theology underlying such interpretations, they often lack the practical tools to challenge these misreadings of the Bible. Perhaps the better preaching strategy is to take advantage of the current cultural interest in apocalyptic themes and help our congregations to interpret Revelation in more responsible ways. What preachers need, then, are clear directions for presenting a faithful and more biblical alternative.

Addressing these practical concerns is the *raison d'etre* for this book. Providing a resource for preachers to engage the latest research and insights into Revelation will hopefully help to remove the most common practical reasons for avoiding

82 Barbara R. Rossing, "The World is About to Turn: Preaching Apocalyptic Texts for a Planet in Peril," in *Eco-Reformation: Grace and Hope for a Planet in Peril*, ed. Lisa E. Dahill, Jim B. Martin-Schramm (Eugene, OR: Wipf and Stock Publishers, 2016), 141.

Revelation.

Revelation and the Lectionary

One of the primary reasons mainline pastors do not preach Revelation more frequently can be laid to its small presence in the Revised Common Lectionary. Simply put, the message of Revelation will not be available to congregations if the preacher consistently follows the lectionary. Those preachers and churches committed to the lectionary will have to make a choice to leave it behind for a season in order to hear Revelation's message:

> The infrequent appearance of Revelation in the *Revised Common Lectionary* aids in that conspiracy of silence. If, however, there is something central to Christian theology in those apocalyptic texts, those texts need to be proclaimed. If the lectionary is not going to help, the preacher needs to do something intentional, such as a sermon series on apocalyptic texts. These texts cannot be left to the Christian fringe.[83]

Departing from the lectionary is not an easy decision for some. It should involve the consent of the congregation leaders, especially if there is a history of lectionary preaching. That decision will put greater burden on any preacher in study and preparation. Resources to help preach lectionary texts are abundant; stray from it and preachers are on their own in sermon and worship preparation. However, engaging Revelation in a substantive way can bring great blessing (Revelation 1:3) and renewal to a congregation. To do so is more work, but it can also provide deep and lasting meaning to parishioners.

One author who advocated preaching a series of sermons on the book of Revelation was Gordon Fee. Fee had many practical suggestions in this regard. His first recommendation was to always preach Revelation as part of a series. Individual sermons on Revelation preached occasionally require too much time to explain the background information that would not need to be

83 Quanbeck II, "Preaching Apocalyptic Texts," 318.

repeated in a series of sermons on the book. Preaching a series can deal substantively with the whole book, treating the entire narrative with seriousness and integrity. While Fee advocated a sermon series as a way to unleash Revelation's voice, he did not recommend a lengthy series. More is not necessarily better. One can lose the grand vision of the forest for the trees when a series is too long.

One of the possibilities Fee recommends is a short, four-week Advent series. Advent and Revelation can make good partners in discussing hope and expectation of Christ's return. Advent, however, is a rather brief season filled with other activities on the parish calendar. The ideal series, says Fee, would last thirteen weeks, perhaps after Easter or in the fall. He suggested the following outline:

1. The introduction(vv. 1-12)
2. The picture of Christ (1:13-20)
3. The seven churches (emphasis on Christ's knowing them)
4. The seven churches (emphasis on their being a mixed bag = reality)
5. Chapters 4-5 (the divine framework for the whole)
6. Chapters 6-7 (the seven seals / two interludes / justice for the martyrs)
7. Chapters 8-10 (God's judgment and evangelism)
8. Chapter 11 (witness and martyrdom / God's final triumph)
9. Chapter 12 (the theology center of the book)
10. Chapter 13-14 (primarily 14: how are we to live in this context)
11. Chapters 17-18 (God's judgments on abuse of power)
12. Chapters 19-20 (God's final judgments on evil and righteous)
13. Chapters 21-22 (the final glory)[84]

The task of a preacher in a series like this is to demonstrate how each section works in the larger framework of Revelation.

This suggestion is commendable on several grounds. First, it pays attention to the whole book of Revelation. A sermon series also provides an opportunity to deal in a comprehensive way with Revelation's symbols and images. A preaching series like this could be profitably accompanied by a weekly teaching series,

---

[84] Gordon D. Fee, "Preaching Apocalyptic? You've Got to Be Kidding!," *Calvin Theological Journal* 41.1 (2006): 15.

thereby reducing the need to take time in the sermon to explain a great deal of historical background.

Lent provides another possibility for preaching Revelation in a series that does not require preachers to leave the lectionary. The season of Lent is the one time of the year when many congregations add a mid-week worship service. Instead of preaching themes being driven by the lectionary, preachers look for a series idea appropriate for the season.

Catherine Gonzalez encourages preachers to launch a preaching series based on the book of Revelation during Lent. Gonzalez detects two distinct missions in the book of Revelation: the mission of Christ and the mission of the church. The mission of Christ is the work of redemption that Christ has won through his death and resurrection. It is the conquest of the demonic powers of sin, death, and the devil. Revelation is filled with songs of praise and thanksgiving for the victory already won by Christ. While the mission of Christ is completed, the mission of the church has only just begun, "to announce the gospel of Christ's victory, not only by its words, but by living as individuals and as a community on the basis that this gospel is true."[85] The church is to persevere in its witness, even in the face of opposition and all evidence to the contrary.

Gonzalez observed that the texts chosen by the lectionary authors for the Easter season of year C are all passages emphasizing the completed mission of Christ.[86] These lessons are certainly appropriate for Easter. What is missing from the lectionary, however, are those passages that emphasize the mission of the church. That mission is the struggle against sin and evil, and giving faithful witness to Christ. These themes are more appropriate for the season of Lent:

> It is in the light of this accomplished victory
> of Jesus and the still to be accomplished mission
> of the church that we need to read the rest of the
> book of Revelation. The two missions interact

85 Catherine Gonzalez, "Mission Accomplished; Mission Begun: Lent and the Book of Revelation," *Journal for Preachers* 32.2 (1999): 9.
86 Revelation 1:4-8; 5:11-14; 7:9-17; 21:1-6; 21:10, 22-22:5; 22:12-14, 16-17, 20-21

constantly throughout the book, so hymns of victory in heaven are alternated with the fury of the battle on earth. The familiar letters to the seven churches in chapters two and three are words of the victorious Christ to churches in Asia Minor whose mission is just beginning. In each there is a call to faithfulness and a promise of victory to those who complete their mission. Each letter begins with a description of the one who speaks, cast in tones of cosmic victory and power. His mission has been accomplished. Theirs is just beginning. The letters point to the particular points at which each church is tempted or shows signs of unfaithfulness. The call is for steadfastness.[87]

Preachers will recognize obvious connections to the traditional themes for Lent in this description. Lent is a season of repentance, a call to struggle against sin, and a call to faithfulness.

The mission of the church needs to be seen as more than a spiritual struggle. Gonzalez argues that unless we discern the first century church's struggle in its historical and political context, we will miss Revelation's message for our own social and political context. The mission of the church is to give witness to Christ even in contexts hostile to the values embodied in the gospel. Gonzalez finds in Revelation 18 a social critique that contrasts the values in the Roman economic system with the gospel:

What is at stake in this passage is the character of the economic system of the Roman Empire, which is not all that different from the system under which we live in terms of its values. It is not only the wealthy who are involved: the whole system of commerce is tied to bringing goods to the wealthy. Even the poorest sailor is tied into this system. The question then is how Christians can live faithfully in an economic system that does not have as its

87 Gonzalez, "Mission Accomplished; Mission Begun: Lent and the Book of Revelation," 10-11.

goal the values of the gospel in terms of loving the neighbor. How does the Christian live under a political system that supports such an economic structure? Granted, the role of the citizen is different today from what it was in the first century Roman Empire, but the question remains for us just as it did for the Christians in John's day.[88]

Lent may be just the perfect time to examine the foundational values of our society in the light of the gospel, and to discern the Christian's role in society. This is exactly the process that John engaged in writing the apocalypse, a "revealing" of the truth about God, the truth about our world, and the truth about the church and its mission in the world.

These issues that challenge the church today are entirely appropriate for conversation and preaching during the season of Lent:

> Lent is an appropriate time to discuss the meaning of discipleship. Discipleship means taking up our cross, following Jesus. If this world remains under the power of evil, then true discipleship will not be easy. Just as Jesus created dissension in his society, so Christians will also be in conflict with elements of their own society. The songs of victory belong to Easter. The times of conflict belong to Lent. The two seasons cannot be separated. Lent is possible only because the first Easter has occurred. But Easter cannot really be celebrated by those who do not understand their own mission as the church of the risen Christ, a mission not yet accomplished. Lent is a time to discuss in study groups as well as in sermons the specifics of what conflict there is between our values as Christians and the values involved in the social, political, and economic systems in which we live.[89]

88 Ibid, 11.
89 Ibid, 12.

Revelation and Lent could be meaningful partners for helping congregations address the central theme of what it means to be the church in our particular time and place.

One of the advantages of a Lenten series on Revelation is that it does not require the preacher to leave the lectionary on Sunday morning. Many churches have a tradition of offering Lenten midweek services. A six-week, midweek series could allow congregations to hear some of the passages from Revelation they have never heard preached before. Another option is to combine Wednesdays and Sunday mornings in an eleven week preaching series on Revelation. This gives even greater opportunity to cover the whole book in a comprehensive way. Because Revelation is a book filled with so much worship, a treasure of hymnody and art exists from which worship planners can creatively draw. Revelation has fired the imagination of countless artists and musicians through the years. Its powerful narrative can inspire the creativity of members in any community.

A further suggestion that could be fruitful in unbinding Revelation is to combine a preaching series with a concurrent Bible study on Revelation. This gives a way for the preacher to convey much historical information, without needing to spend valuable time doing that in the sermon. It also gives the congregation a way to interact with the text and ask the questions that inevitably arise when studying Revelation. One resource the author has found extremely helpful is the book, *Come, Lord Jesus: A Study of Revelation*, by Mark Braaten.[90] Mark is a Lutheran pastor who wrote the book for interested laypeople. The book engages recent scholarship on Revelation in a way that is accessible and readable.

One final suggestion that will help congregations to interact with Revelation is to do an oral enactment or dramatic reading of the text. This experience of hearing the whole book in one sitting could be a one-time event, or part of a worship/preaching series on Revelation. That is the subject of Chapter 4.

90 Mark Braaten, *Come, Lord Jesus: A Study of Revelation* (Collegeville, MN: Liturgical Press, 2007, 2018 2nd edition).

General Homiletical Strategies for Preaching Revelation

Having addressed several internal and external reasons preachers avoid the book of Revelation, I would like to summarize much of the preceding chapters and highlight a few general characteristics for preaching from Revelation. These homiletical strategies explore the relationship of Christ and culture, the principalities and powers, and envisioning the new creation.

Christ and Culture / Church and State

While many commentators acknowledge the importance of responsible and faithful preaching of Revelation, many of them, however, only point the way in rather broad and general strokes:

> Two reasons why Revelation can and should speak to people today can be summed up around the poles of Christ and culture.... Although Christians in the west may not be preoccupied with questions about eating meat offered to idols, many are aware of contemporary pressures to relinquish one's faith commitments because of the appeal of assimilating into the wider culture, the complacency that arises from prosperity, or the threat of violence. As modern readers confront such issues, Revelation continues to challenge and encourage them.[91]

Exploring the relationship between Christ and culture can be fruitful in understanding how Revelation can speak to the church today.

The relationship between Christ and culture, or church and culture, is a complex one, but helpful to examine when it comes to interpreting and preaching Revelation. Evidence of a debate around this relationship exists in the churches to whom John wrote. Craig Koester identifies three groups within the early church that heard the message of Revelation in distinctly different ways: complacent Christians who benefited from their unquestioning participation in the dominant culture, Christians who were being tempted to assimilate into that culture, and

91 Koester, *Revelation and the End of All Things*, 202-3.

Christians who refused to participate in the secular culture for ethical and religious reasons. In lifting up this variety of responses, preachers can find echoes that speak across the centuries to issues many Christians struggle with today. Preachers also avoid the misunderstanding that Revelation was only written to a community undergoing persecution and therefore, is unable to speak powerfully to the affluent congregations they serve.

One of the recent studies exploring the relationship of Christ and culture in a more nuanced way is Walter Pilgrim's book, *Uneasy Neighbors: Church and State in the New Testament*. Pilgrim argues that the New Testament does not contain one unified response to the relationship of church and state, but three different and at times conflicting responses. The first he called the ethic of subordination, which draws heavily upon Pauline traditions, especially Romans 13. This ethic represents the predominant New Testament attitude for the majority of Christians. "This tradition regards the government as God's gift to preserve and promote the public good - peace, order, justice, freedom, and human dignity. In response Christians give to the state their respect, obedience, support, and prayers. In this view, the church and state can and should coexist as mutually supportive."[92] Pilgrim maintained that for many Christians this is the only ethical stance toward the state.

The second response or attitude toward the state Pilgrim calls the ethic of critical distancing, which he finds in the gospels and their characterization of Jesus' own relationship to the state. Jesus' relationship with the ruling authorities was not one of subordination, neither was it that of the zealot or political revolutionary:

> The Jesus of the gospels is no servile subject to those who rule. Although he accepts the political order, his allegiance is to God and God alone. Accordingly, his life from beginning to end is a history of conflict with those in power…. He criticizes those who abuse and misuse their power,

92 Walter E. Pilgrim, *Uneasy Neighbors: Church and State in the New Testament*. Overtures to Biblical Theology (Minneapolis, MN: Fortress Press, 1999), 36.

wealth, and position. He allows the tax to Caesar but along with it calls for a higher obedience to the things of God. He persists in his preaching of the kingdom to the very end, despite the growing opposition and hostility from those in authority.[93]

Pilgrim argued that Jesus' attitude toward the state was distinct from the ethic of subordination one finds in Pauline literature.

> Jesus' way, therefore, is not that of simple subordination to those who rule. Noticeably absent is any call to pray for rulers or emperors or to honor and respect them as servants appointed by God.... But neither does one find overt hostility toward rulers per se nor any description of the imperial state as the demonic manifestation of evil on earth or as the great anti-Christ, as we will find in Revelation.... While Jesus accepts the necessary role of those who govern, he stands as a constant critic of the political and religious establishment, even daring ultimately to provoke it to change, at the risk of his own life."[94]

An ethic of critical distancing seeks to engage the powers that be in an effort to bring about change for greater justice.

The third response to the state Pilgrim calls the ethic of resistance, which comes primarily from the book of Revelation. In Revelation, the church and the Roman Empire are treated as mortal enemies:

> The apocalypse adopts a stance toward the state that is radically different from the two other New Testament traditions. Here we find an understanding of the political structures as demonic, historical embodiments of injustice and evil. In response, the church is encouraged toward an ethic of uncompromising resistance....

93 Ibid, 123.
94 Ibid, 124.

Revelation, I argue, does not teach an escapist ethic of irresponsibility toward history. Instead, it intends to motivate and encourage action toward greater justice on behalf of suffering believers and all humanity. And though it advocates resistance, it is nonviolent resistance patterned after the suffering of the lamb who was slain, the central Christological image in Revelation.[95]

Here, the appropriate ethic of the church toward the state is uncompromising resistance to an evil status-quo on behalf of a more just future.

Pilgrim concluded his book by advocating a contextual ethic based on how well the state fulfills its divine mandate to promote the common good. The church and state live in uneasy tension with each other:

> The church rejects all idolatrous claims of the state as demonic. Some of these claims are relatively easy to discern: emperor worship, twentieth century tyrannical governments (Nazism, Stalinism, Maoism, apartheid). Other idolatrous claims and injustices are more subtle: reliance on military power, unjust wars, economic exploitation, violation of human rights, racial/gender inequalities, ecological abuses. It is the task of the church, as God's representative in the world, to discern the particular temptation or injustice at work and then to take its stand based on its biblical, theological, ethical, and prayerful grasp of the times and situation.[96]

Deciding which ethical stance to adopt in specific historical situations is a communal task of discernment.

Two authors who apply this ethic of resistance specifically to the task of preaching Revelation today are Stanley Saunders and Charles Campbell. Saunders argues that seeing Revelation

95 Ibid, 178.
96 Ibid, 186-7.

as resistance literature has direct consequences for the church's worship and proclamation:

> [The book of Revelation] is, in other words, a prime example of a narrative of resistance, a work designed to create imaginative space for discourse and social practice that pose a sharp alternative to 'empire.' Revelation was created for oral performance amid the eucharistic gatherings of the early Christians.... Revelation, in fact, presents worship itself as the definitive act of Christian resistance against the idolatry and violence of Roman imperial domination. The apocalypse as a whole also represents a particularly interesting expression of early Christian proclamation, directed apparently both to those who suffered and those who prospered under Roman imperial ideology and practice.[97]

Preaching and worship, as modeled in Revelation, embodied values that were counter to Roman culture and ideology.

Campbell considers this understanding of Revelation as resistance literature to be particularly helpful for preachers in privileged congregations who may wonder what word, if any, Revelation has to speak to them:

> When understood through the lens of resistance, however, Revelation becomes more accessible to such preachers. For marginalized, persecuted groups, the apocalypse may indeed fashion resistance to oppression and help people endure in the midst of suffering. For privileged groups, the call to resistance may be just as strong, though in this context congregations will be challenged to "come out" of the empire that has seduced us by

97 Stanley P. Saunders, "Revelation and Resistance: Narrative and Worship in John's Apocalypse," *In Narrative Reading, Narrative Preaching: Reuniting New Testament Interpretation and Proclamation,* ed. Joel B. Green and Michael Pasquarello (Grand Rapids, MI: Baker Academic, 2003), 118.

its values (18:4) and to resist accommodation to the ways of the "powers that be."[98]

How one preaches the book of Revelation, then, is greatly influenced by one's own socio-political location and theological perspective.

Greg Carey shared this conviction that the preacher's social location shapes how he or she will preach and teach Revelation today.[99] Revelation, he said, does not teach us lessons as much as it asks us questions. It challenges us to locate ourselves in relation to our own culture and identify those places where repentance is needed.

Carey claimed that Revelation offers three distinct modes of address to its audience: comfort, exhortation and admonition. These three modes reflect the diversity of audience to whom John was writing. Comfort was offered to those who were struggling to be faithful. Exhortation was given to those trying to discern how to engage the surrounding culture. Admonition was spoken to those who were part of a comfortable status quo that had accommodated to the values of the dominant culture. One sees these three modes most clearly in the letters to the seven churches, but John skillfully weaves all three together throughout Revelation, thereby giving his audience multiple places to see itself in the story. If Revelation forced its original audience to grapple with the question of its relationship to the dominant culture, the book certainly confronts modern audiences with the same question.

In any culture, there are deep divisions separating people who disagree with each other. There is evidence that this was the case among the Christian communities of John's time. Some Christian leaders advocated accommodation with Roman culture. Opposing this, John called Christians to repent and "come out" of Babylon. John was uncompromising in his assessment of Rome as an evil empire. Contemporary Christians may hear his voice as a call to discernment, and a call to think critically about society and their involvement in it:

98 Campbell, "Apocalypse Now: Preaching Revelation as Narrative." 152-3.
99 Carey, "Teaching and Preaching the Book of Revelation in the Church."

The most appropriate response for contemporary disciples may be to drop the attempt to link the beast with a single social, religious, or political reality; instead, we might ask what is beastly about our own society. This challenge involves not so much labeling culture as analyzing it. Proclamation and teaching, then, would require prophetic engagement and public discernment.[100]

For Carey, the church must live and struggle with the question of its relationship to culture. A critical evaluation of society is what Christians are called to engage in.

A valuable tool in this critical engagement with culture is the biblical concept of principalities and powers. Referred to earlier is the work of Walter Wink. These principalities and powers that live in rebellion to God seek to enslave humanity by using tactics of fear or seduction. Charles Campbell gives a modern day example of the seductive reach of the powers:

> Here one is reminded of the power of global capitalism, embodied in enormous corporations that seek dominion over the world, not primarily through physical threats, but through the seduction of our spirits through advertising and consumerism. Such seduction shapes the lives of countless people today, including those in our churches, who consume and consume and consume, even though we know it is killing us and we know it is killing others who work in sweatshops around the world. Yet we often seem powerless to resist; we almost seem to be possessed. Such is the seductive lure of the principalities and powers. And when they succeed in seducing us, they no longer need to use threats.[101]

This is the context into which many mainline preachers today will need to translate the book of Revelation. For many, that may be a daunting task:

100 Ibid, 94.
101 Campbell, "Apocalypse Now: Preaching Revelation as Narrative." 156.

Revelation is not a book for therapeutic preachers who wish simply to address the needs and problems of individual congregation members. It is a book that invites preachers into the public, political arena…. That fact, even more than the bizarre imagery and obscure metaphors, may present the greatest challenge to Christian preachers today, pushing us to come to terms with our own captivity to the principalities and powers.[102]

Campbell points modern preachers of Revelation in one further direction. Not only does Revelation reveal the deadly ways of the powers that be, it also envisions a new creation that embraces God's justice and peace. "Here too, John employs dramatic, audacious 'big pictures' that engage the congregation's imagination, give people hope, and empower the community to begin living now in God's new creation."[103] Giving voice to that new creation is the first step to shattering old realities and evoking new possibilities in the congregation.

102 Ibid, 157.
103 Ibid, 161.

Sermons On The Book Of Revelation

*"Let Anyone Who Has An Ear Listen
To What The Spirit Is Saying To The Churches"*

The following sermons were all preached in the fall of 2018 in the congregation I was serving. They are an attempt to preach these texts in the context of my own community and current events. I do not include them here as examples of good sermons, but they will certainly point the way and give busy preachers a foundation to create their own sermons with their own style. Many of the stories in these sermons are personal. I hope they will inspire preachers to find and tell their own stories.

#1 — It's All About Jesus: Revelation 1:4-6, 9-18

Spring Valley and Spring Grove- do you ever get the two cities mixed up? I do all the time. Soon after I arrived in Harmony, I had a pastor's meeting in Spring Grove. It was a beautiful day and I was enjoying the weather - until I ended up in Spring Valley and realized I had arrived at the wrong town. When I left Harmony, I drove north on Main Street three blocks to the highway. Which way do I turn - left or right? The decision of where to turn began in my head. My assumptions about where this meeting was supposed to be landed me in a totally wrong place.

The same thing happens when many people read the book of Revelation. They assume that it contains predictions about the end-times, and that we are living in them. They assume that the things described in Revelation are events we are experiencing now, and that the end is near. But to read Revelation that way is like ending up in Spring Valley when you are supposed to end up in Spring Grove.

I want to say a few things about how we read this fascinating book. First, we read it much the same way we read any other book of the Bible. We ask questions about what it meant when it was first written, and only then do we begin to ask what it might mean for us today. When we read the book of Romans, we don't assume that the apostle Paul was writing to Christians living 2,000 years in the distant future. We shouldn't do that with Revelation either. The book of Revelation does not reveal an end-time calendar; it reveals Jesus Christ. In fact, those are the very first words of the book. "The revelation of Jesus Christ." This book is all about revealing Christ to Christians who lived in Asia Minor 1,900 years ago. The amazing thing is that those words still speak to Christians today with power and insight and bring blessing into our lives.

The second thing we need to know is that John used symbols to communicate important spiritual truths. John didn't mean what he said, he meant what he meant. So when John talked about Jesus having a sword coming from his mouth, he was not talking about a literal sword. That's absurd. Jesus was no sword-swallower in a circus act. No, we have to ask what John meant. The sword is a symbol to show us the power of the word of God. We talk about spoken words that cut to the quick or that are cutting remarks. It's the same symbol here.

Two years ago, I had the privilege of serving as a volunteer chaplain for two weeks in Wittenberg, Germany, home of Martin Luther and the birthplace of the Reformation. Worship was held in the sacristy, a large room just off of the chancel. There on the wall, just behind the lectern, was a large sandstone relief. On it was a picture of Christ, the judge of the world. There was a sword coming from his mouth. It was part of the piety of the time before the Reformation, and it was meant to scare people as they came for worship and warn them not to fall asleep during the sermon. Luther disliked this image. He much preferred to focus on Christ as Savior, instead of Christ as judge.

This picture of Christ as judge comes straight from the first chapter of Revelation. The prophet John saw the glorified Christ. "I saw one like the Son of Man, clothed with a long robe... In his right hand he held seven stars, and from his mouth came a sharp, two-edged sword, and his face was like the sun shining with full force." It's interesting that John's reaction was to fall at Jesus' feet as though dead. He was terrified! But what was Jesus' immediate response to him? He placed his hand on him and said, "Don't be afraid. I am the first and the last, and the living one. I was dead, and see, I am alive forever and ever; and I have the keys of death and Hades." Jesus reached out in compassion to John and told him not to fear. And Jesus is saying the same thing to us today, "Don't be afraid." Don't be afraid of this book and its strange and bizarre images. Revelation is the only book in the Bible that contains a promised blessing for those who read it.

A sword coming from Jesus' mouth can be a rather frightening symbol until we understand what it means. Hebrews 4:12-13 says that "the word of God is living and active, sharper than any two-edged sword, piercing until it divides soul from spirit, joints from marrow; it is able to judge the thoughts and intentions of the heart. And before him no creature is hidden, but all are naked and laid bare to the eyes of the one to whom we must render an account." God's word is powerful. That's what this symbol means. We can't hide from God. The word of God pierces to the center of who we are, where soul meets spirit. There are no masks God can't look behind, no secret sins God doesn't see.

The word of God cuts into us, past all our defenses and past everything that defines us to show us the truth about who we are. Who are you? You are a mother or father, a son or daughter. You are a student or employee or retired volunteer. Who are you? You are the sum of all your accomplishments and failures in life, your hopes and dreams and disappointments. You are all these things, and yet you are more than these things. The word of God cuts through all the layers of your identity to get to you, just you. God's word twists you open so that the core of who you are is laid bare and exposed. The word of God cuts through all your illusions and tells you the truth about who you are. We are broken and flawed people in desperate need of a Savior.

If the risen Christ reveals who we are, we must remember that there are two edges to this sword. The word of God also reveals whose we are. The word of God not only shows us our sins, but also shows us a Savior, who loves us. "To him who loves us and freed us from our sins by his blood." In baptism, we are declared children of God. God claims us and gives us a new identity.

Many of you are familiar with the *Chronicles of Narnia* series by C.S. Lewis. They are children's fantasy with a message to teach spiritual truths. One of my favorite stories is in the book, *The Voyage of the Dawn Treader*. It was made into a movie in 2010. The book introduces us to a young boy named Eustace. Eustace was a brat who didn't care about anyone except Eustace. He enjoyed bullying and bossing anyone he could. You get the idea that no one much liked Eustace. In one adventure, Eustace ignored everyone's warnings and wandered off to explore an island. He stumbled across a dragon's lair filled with gold. Eustace couldn't believe his luck. He settled in to count his new-found gold and fell asleep. When he woke up, he found that he had become a dragon. Eustace was horrified at what he had become, so much so that he began to despair and wonder what would ever happen to him. It was then, when Eustace was willing to look deep inside himself and acknowledge the truth of who he was, that he had an encounter with Aslan, the ruler of Narnia. Eustace described what happened next. "I looked up and saw the very last thing I expected: a huge lion coming slowly towards me…. You may think that, being a dragon, I could have knocked any lion out easily enough. But it wasn't that kind of fear. I wasn't afraid of it eating me, I was just afraid of it — if you understand. Well, it came closer up to me and looked straight into my eyes. And I shut my eyes tight. But that wasn't any good because it told me to follow it…. And I knew that I would have to do what it told me, so I got up and followed it."

The lion led Eustace to a pool of water and told him to undress. Eustace tried to shed his dragon skin by scraping away its scales. He tried three times and failed. It was then that the lion said, "You will have to let me undress you." Eustace continued his story. "I was afraid of his claws, I can tell you, but I was pretty nearly desperate now. So I just lay flat down on my back and let him do it. The very first tear he made was so deep that I thought it had gone right into my heart. And when he began pulling the skin off, it hurt worse than anything I've ever felt. The only thing that made me able to bear it was just the pleasure of feeling the stuff peel off…. Well, he peeled the beastly stuff right off…. Then he caught hold of me …and threw me into the water. It smarted like anything but only for a moment. After that it became perfectly delicious and as soon as I started swimming and splashing, I found that… I'd turned into a boy again."[104]

A lion's claw, a two-edged sword- two symbols that point to the same reality, the power of God to free us from our sins, our addictions and idolatries. Throughout Revelation John will do that again and again, reveal the true nature of things and invite us to follow Jesus, to worship God alone.

Christ is coming to each one of us, speaking to us his powerful word, cutting deep into our hearts to reveal who we really are, and also whose we are. We are beloved children of God, freed from our sins, called to follow Jesus.

> Suggested Prayer of the Day — ELW Transfiguration C
> Suggested Opening Hymn — "Crown Him with Many Crowns"
> Suggested Hymn of the Day — "Shine, Jesus, Shine"
> Suggested Closing Hymn — "Shout to the Lord"

#2 — Seven Letters; Three Messages: Revelation 2:1-7; 3:14-22

When I was in college, I took up pipe smoking. I was a philosophy minor, and I thought it looked rather cool and sophisticated. While I enjoyed the smell of pipe tobacco, I never really enjoyed smoking all that much. So, it surprised me one day when I got a letter in the mail from my father. He had come to visit me at college the week before and discovered the pipe in my dorm room. Dad was very disappointed and even angered that I would start smoking, and so he wrote the letter to express

---

104 Clive Staples Lewis, *The Voyage of the Dawn Treader* (Boston, MA: Wyatt North Publishing, 2002).

his displeasure. In the letter he asked me to throw the pipe away and promise to quit smoking or he would refuse to pay for my last year of college. You have to understand that my father was an educator and school principal. He had crusaded for years against smoking. No son of his was going to smoke, especially one whose college tuition he was paying for. So I wrote my father a response. "My smoking wasn't a big deal. I didn't do it very much, and when I did, I didn't inhale! Don't worry, Dad." My father was not impressed. He wrote me a second letter and said that he wanted a signed letter from me promising not to smoke, and he wanted the letter notarized. My father was playing hardball. Even though he was stern with me, I knew that the real reason he was doing this was because he loved me. I think he was even proud of me.

The letters to the seven churches in Revelation function in a similar way to that. The prophet John was very familiar with each church and cared deeply about them. They were real churches in real communities facing unique circumstances. He wrote to encourage them, to warn them not to compromise their faith, and where they were wrong, to call them to change their ways. He was in many ways like a parent writing to children he loved to encourage and admonish them.

I think that when many people think about Revelation, they think it was written to people undergoing persecution for their faith. And while that was true for some, it is not the whole story. Persecution of Christians at that time was not widespread. In general, the issues facing these seven churches fall into three basic categories. There were those churches that were being persecuted for their faith. There were churches who were being tempted to adopt Roman and pagan ways in order to get ahead. And there were those churches that had become so complacent and comfortable with Roman ways that they had lost their distinct Christian identity.

Think of these seven letters like a stoplight with three different lights: green, yellow, and red. The churches suffering persecution got a green light from John. He encouraged them to continue to persevere and keep the faith. John gave a yellow light to those churches that were being tempted to adopt Roman ways. He gave them a warning and urged caution in becoming too much like the surrounding pagan culture. And to the churches that were comfortable with Roman ways, John gave a red light. Stop! Change direction, because the road you are on will not bring you God's blessing.

One of the main questions facing these early Christians was how much to participate in the surrounding Roman culture. Many of the cities John was writing to had temples devoted to the worship of various gods or goddesses. Some of them had temples devoted to Caesar worship. During the year, there would be civic festivals celebrating various gods or Caesar. Animals would be sacrificed, and meat was consumed. Was it okay for Christians to eat that meat? Could they participate in the parades? Often worshipers would come to the temple of their gods with animals to be sacrificed. The meat that wasn't consumed would often end up being sold in the marketplace. Could Christians eat that meat that had been sacrificed to an idol? Many cities had social and trade associations, much like our civic organizations today like the Jaycees, Chamber of Commerce, or Rotary Club. Many of those associations had a patron deity and had religious elements to their meetings. Was it okay for Christian business owners to participate in those associations when the worship of other gods was involved? For many of them, not doing so would put them at economic disadvantage. Do you begin to understand some of the real issues facing these first century Christians?

Let me give you another example. Fillmore County, Minnesota, home to about 1,000 Old Order Amish. The Amish have chosen a distinctive lifestyle because of their religious beliefs. There are many ways in which they have chosen not to participate in the surrounding culture. They deal with questions of assimilation every day. How far can they go in associating with the "English" and yet still be faithful to their beliefs? There have been times when the local bishop has had to discipline some of the members who have strayed too far. The Amish don't participate in any of our civic organizations, don't send their children to our schools and don't pledge allegiance to the flag. Despite this, many of us "English" have good relationships with the Amish. They often help each other out. Some businesses runs Amish tours for visitors who are curious about the Amish and their lifestyle. That is the predominant attitude many people have toward them- curiosity. But what if we were a religious society and the Amish refusal to participate was seen as disloyal and unpatriotic? We would look at them with suspicion and distrust. We would view them as second-class citizens. And when that happens, it is an easy step to begin persecuting them.

That was the situation facing the Christians to whom John was writing. John saw that there were three basic ways Christians had chosen to participate in the surrounding Roman culture. Some refused altogether and were viewed with suspicion as disloyal and unpatriotic. To them John wrote words of commendation and encouragement to remain faithful. Other Christians were being tempted to assimilate to Roman ways, and John wrote them words of warning. You cannot serve God and Rome. Other Christians had made peace with Rome and lost the distinctiveness of their Christian faith. To them John wrote words of condemnation and called on them to change.

We don't live in ancient Rome and we aren't Amish. But aren't there ways today in which Christians are tempted to compromise their faith in order to participate in society? Our gods today aren't in the form of ancient idols, but they are every bit as real. So many of us today worship at the altar of wealth or power. We bow before idols of race or nationalism. We put ourselves on the altar of pleasure and self-indulgence. But at what price? Do we sell our souls to the devil in order to become rich? Do we believe lies and perpetuate fake news because it makes us feel good about ourselves? We love our country, but we worship a God that loves all countries, "every tribe and language and people and nation." In our baptism we are called to "serve all people, following the example of our Lord Jesus, and to strive for justice and peace in all the earth." When do we stand up and say "no!" to unjust systems? When do we refuse to compromise our faith in order to just get along?

John has a word for Christians living today. That word is a call to be faithful. Jesus says to us today just like he said to the church in Laodicea, "I reprove and discipline those whom I love. Be earnest, therefore and repent. Listen! I am standing at the door, knocking; if you hear my voice and open the door, I will come into you and eat with you and you with me." Jesus reminds us that we are loved and we are not alone in our struggles.

There is one thing that John said to all seven churches. He gave them all a promise and encouragement to conquer. To the church in Ephesus John said, "To everyone who conquers, I will give permission to eat from the tree of life that is in the paradise of God." And to the church in Laodicea, John said, "To the one who conquers I will give a place with me on my throne, just as I myself conquered and sat down with my Father on his throne." John was intentional in using that word "conquer." John was using a word that was a favorite of the Romans. Rome loved to conquer. It celebrated victory in battle. Victory was celebrated as a winged goddess. Her image was everywhere, on flags and statues and building facades, even imprinted on coins. Everywhere you went in the Roman Empire, the message was loud and clear — Romans were winners and the gods were "on their side."

But John had a very different idea about the word "conquer." Rome hasn't conquered; Jesus the lamb that was slaughtered has conquered. And those who follow the lamb will also conquer. John explains how in chapter 12. "They have conquered ...by the blood of the lamb and by the word of their testimony, for they did not cling to life even in the face of death." What John is doing here is offering a counter to Rome's worship of military power and violence. Christians conquer, not by military power, but by the power of the lamb who was slain. Christians conquer by their testimony to the life-giving power of God, and the grace God so freely gives us in Jesus Christ. Christians speak truth to power when that power is built on lies and injustice. Christians give testimony to the new life God invites us to even when their own lives are being threatened.

We are faced with many temptations in our world today to compromise our faith in order to get along. Either we are afraid to rock the boat, or we are seduced by promises of wealth into accepting the status quo. Either way, our silence and complicity in society is what is demanded of us. Today, John is reminding us that the lamb has conquered. We who follow the lamb will conquer also as we give testimony to the lamb and to the new future God is bringing to our world. Amen.

Suggested Prayer of the Day — ELW p. 72 "Before Worship"
Suggested Opening Hymn — "All Hail the Power of Jesus' Name"
Suggested Hymn of the Day — "Spirit of God, Descend Upon My Heart"
Suggested Closing Hymn — "Lord of Glory, You Have Bought Us"

#3 — Worship That is Out of This World: Revelation 4:1-11

A couple of years ago, my wife and I were traveling in Norway and had the opportunity to visit the royal palace in the capital city, Oslo. It's a large beautiful building. And though not as opulent and luxurious as other palaces in Europe, it is still impressive. Norway is a constitutional monarchy, much like England, so the royals don't have any real power, though they certainly have influence. Kings and queens just aren't what they used to be. Our attitude toward them today is very different than what it was in biblical times. Back then rulers were absolute. They could do whatever they wanted. And they often did.

One of the most important rooms in a palace was the throne room. This was the place where the king met the public and emissaries from other countries. The throne room was where kings displayed their wealth and power. When you entered the room and saw the wealth, you were supposed to be intimidated and humbled into submission. This was the place where loyalty was pledged and devotion to the king was given.

In Revelation chapter 4, John took us on a private tour of a palace and throne room that was literally out of this world. It was an amazing place he described. "There in heaven stood a throne, with one seated on the throne." God is described looking like rare jewels and a rainbow. Flashes of lightning and thunder came from the throne, surrounded by a sea of glass like crystal. And God is not alone in the throne room. There are the four living creatures who never cease their song of praise. "Holy, holy, holy, the Lord God the almighty, who was and is and is to come." And then there are the 24 elders who fall before the throne to worship God. They take off their crowns and cast them before the throne singing, "You are worthy, our Lord and God, to receive glory and honor and power, for you created all things, and by your will they existed and were created." Now, if we scratch our heads and try to figure out who all these creatures are, we are going to miss the impact John wants this scene to have on us. John wants us to be awed and amazed, blown away by the incredible glory and majesty of God. John gives us a glimpse into the deepest reality in the universe that is meant to get us to bow our knees and hearts before God in utter worship and adoration.

When you read this chapter, there is music all over the place. You can hardly read it without breaking into song. Chapters 4 and 5 of Revelation have inspired so many of our hymns and contemporary songs and liturgy. One of my favorites is that great hymn, "Love Divine, All Loves Excelling". The last verse comes straight from Revelation. "Changed from glory into glory, Till in heav'n we take our place, Till we cast our crowns before thee, Lost in wonder, love, and praise!" Lost in wonder, love, and praise- that is exactly what John wants to happen in us.

Revelation is all about worshiping God. Again and again, it tells us to worship God and refuse to worship lesser gods. And in order to have the strength to remain faithful, John calls us to worship. There is this pattern in Revelation. We begin with worship in chapters 4 and 5, and then in chapter 6 the seven seals are opened. Tragedies strike the earth. But before the seventh seal is broken there is an interlude and in chapter 7 we are taken back up to heaven to experience worship. That same pattern happens again in chapters 8 and 9 with the seven trumpets and terrible trials on earth. But before the seventh trumpet sounds there is another interlude and we are again taken up to heaven. It's not an accident that, again and again, Revelation returns us to worship. It's like the third commandment — six days you shall work but the seventh is a day of rest and worship. Week after week we need worship to sustain us. I don't know about you, but six days is about as long as I want to go before being reminded again in worship that I truly am loved and my sins are forgiven. You see, the world has a way of beating us up. At times, our troubles and problems can seem to overwhelm us. We can become discouraged and lost. What worship does is lift us out of ourselves and our problems and take us up to heaven to see things from God's perspective. It gives us strength to resist the temptations that come our way. Worship gives us encouragement when we want to give up. If you want to know how to survive in today's world, John has one word for us — worship!

Have you ever had a near-death experience? I've known a few people who have. And the one thing they always say is how the experience has changed them. They are no longer afraid to die. They see themselves and life differently. They no longer live in fear, but in faith. It changes how they live day to day. That's the same thing worship does for us. It lifts us out of ourselves and helps us look at ourselves, our problems, and our world differently.

Let me give you another example. Most people today love a good movie. Movies can be an escape. And sometimes they give us a new perspective. We go back to our daily life changed. We see things differently. We see the mundane circumstances of our everyday lives differently. Take, for instance, the movie, *Unbroken*. It was about a WWII soldier who endured incredible torture at the hands of his Japanese captors. After the war, he returned home troubled by the post-traumatic stress that almost destroyed his life. It was in an encounter with Christ that he found peace. Eventually, he returned to Japan to meet his former captors and extend them forgiveness. When you see a movie like that, it gives you new perspective. Those one to two hours change you and how you view life. If this soldier who experienced that can learn how to forgive, so can you.

That is what worship will do for you. It gives you a new perspective to see things through God's eyes. Maybe you came here today, wondering how you are going to make it. Maybe you are here today not even sure if you even believe in God. John has a recommendation for you — worship God! Get your eyes off yourself and onto the King of kings.

There is another dimension to worship that we need to notice. In verse eleven, John described the 24 elders before the throne of God singing a song of praise. "You are worthy, our Lord and God..." In describing worship that way, John is making a political statement. He is deliberately using the language from the cult of emperor worship and changing it to send a message. Roman citizens would demonstrate their patriotism and loyalty by kneeling before a statue of Caesar, offering a pinch of incense, and calling Caesar "our Lord and God". To that John said, "No!" Only God deserves that title.

Here's another way of looking at it. Suppose someone says to you, "I pledge allegiance to the...." You expect to hear the word "flag." But what if I said to you, "I pledge allegiance to the lamb"? That is a deliberate change that is meant to jar your expectations. One word changes the meaning. By changing that one word, I am sending a message that there is a higher loyalty than flag and country, and it is our loyalty to God. That was exactly what John did here in Revelation. He used the language of the empire to say that Caesar was not God. There is only one worthy of our worship and praise. Saying yes to God meant saying no to Caesar. There is a higher loyalty in my life, and when Caesar is wrong, I must say "no" and follow God.

And it's all set to music. Let me give you an example out of our own nation's history. The Negro spirituals grew out of slavery and the experience of an oppressed people. They were songs not only to inspire hope and faith, but also to galvanize resistance to the fact that Blacks were considered sub-human. The song, "We Shall Overcome," comes right out of Revelation. That's the power of worship. It gives us the strength to resist idolatrous claims no matter where they come from, whether it's ancient Rome, Nazi Germany, South African Apartheid, or even our own government.

Our ancient Christian brothers and sisters found the courage to say "no" to Caesar. They refused to worship Caesar. They would be good citizens in every other way, but they refused to worship Caesar. For that, they were accused of being disloyal and unpatriotic. They were treated as second-class people. They were refused social and economic advantages that other Roman citizens enjoyed. And they were persecuted and sometimes killed because of their faith. We can learn a lot from their example.

When you are feeling frightened, when you are feeling confused, when you are consumed with your problems, when you don't know how you're going to make it, listen for a voice inviting you, "Come up here. Let me show you the throne room of the King of kings." We worship an awesome God, creator of heaven and earth. There, standing at the door is Jesus, waiting to eat with you. He gives us himself, the water of life and fruit from the tree of life for our healing. And just like the 24 elders, we are invited to cast our crowns before him. Worship God and get your eyes off of yourself and your problems, your cares and worries. Lose yourself in wonder, love, and praise. Amen.

Suggested Prayer of the Day — ELW p. 37 Holy Trinity #1
Suggested Opening Hymn — "Immortal, Invisible, God Only Wise"
Suggested Hymn of the Day — "Holy God, We Praise Your Name"
Suggested Closing Hymn — "Love Divine, All Loves Excelling"

#4 — The Power of the Lamb: Revelation 5:1-14

In the fall of 1982, I spent a semester in Germany at a German language school. I had a room in a private home. Since most of my meals were eaten at school or in restaurants, I rarely saw my host. But there was one meal a week that I shared with the family — Saturday breakfast. Mostly we had good conversations as they tried to make this foreigner feel welcome. But sometimes the conversation would turn to politics. When they spoke about the WW2 and Hitler, I heard a whole new way of viewing history. For me, raised and educated in the United States, Hitler was the embodiment of evil. But they didn't see him that way at all. Hitler had done good things for the German people, restoring their pride and rebuilding the nation, putting people back to work. To them Hitler had been *Der Führer,* a wise and benevolent leader. He offered a vision of the future that was compelling to many Germans who were impoverished in the aftermath of World War 1. At the time, many saw him as the savior of Germany come to establish a perfect state — the Third Reich. *"Heil Hitler!"* was the Nazi salute, and it meant literally, "salvation to Hitler." It was a ritual that unified Germans. It impacted every part of public life. The Hitler salute showed one's loyalty and allegiance to Hitler and his vision for the future. To refuse to give the Hitler salute was to invite suspicion and persecution. Many Germans followed Hitler with blind and unquestioning loyalty, and they truly believed in the glorious future he would bring them. It wasn't until after the war that most Germans learned just how blind they had been. When the concentration camps were emptied, the world learned that it wasn't salvation that *Der Führer* had come to bring.

What makes a good leader? What we look for in a leader says a lot about who we are, and about what our hopes and dreams are. Every four years the people of the United States go through the process of electing a president. We have a national struggle to define the kind of person we want to lead us. What we look for in a leader depends on what kind of future we envision for our country. It is all part of the process of trying to create a "more perfect union." And when times are difficult, we look for an individual with special gifts to lead the nation. We may look for qualities of intelligence, morals, or faith. Do we need an expert in business who can restore the economy? Do we need a strong military leader who can guarantee our security and status in the world? Who will make our lives better? Who will get us to the promised land?

These hopes and dreams are common to all people. How are we going to create a better world, and who can help us create that better world? The answer to that question is what the prophet John shares with us in Chapter 5. "Then I saw in the right hand of the one seated on the throne a scroll... sealed with seven seals." Most scholars believe that the scroll represents God's plan for the redemption of the world, a plan to establish God's reign of justice and peace on the earth. John sees a mighty angel asking the question, "Who is worthy to open the scroll and break its seals?" In other words, who will accomplish God's plan? Who will establish peace and justice throughout the earth? Who will lead us to a better world? John broke into tears when he learned that "no one in heaven or on earth or under the earth was able to open the scroll or to look into it." No human being had the knowledge or skill. No human being was capable or worthy. None.

You and I living today in the United States might hear that and yawn. What's the big deal? But to Christians living back then in the Roman Empire, this statement was deeply political. Rome offered a compelling vision for the world. The Roman emperors were worshiped as divine saviors of the world. They brought peace on earth. People hailed Caesar as lord and god. Roman propaganda was filled with images showing the gods on Rome's side and touting the benefits of Roman rule. Rome boasted of its military power and that it alone could conquer the world and guarantee peace. That propaganda saturated every aspect of life in the ancient world — religious, political, social, and economic. It was a vision that many people bought into. Temples for emperor worship were erected in three of the seven cities that John wrote to. Emperor worship was part of the glue that held the empire together. But, according to John, it was all a lie. Caesar was not the savior of the world. In fact, no one was found worthy to accomplish God's will and create a better world. Not Caesar — Not anyone!

At this, John described how he began to weep bitterly. People need hope that somehow the future will be better than the past.

They need to believe that someone, somewhere is capable of solving their problems and making the world a better place. This is particularly true of people experiencing oppression. But then John said that he heard a loud voice. "Do not weep. See, the lion of the tribe of Judah, the root of David, has conquered, so that he can open the scroll and its seven seals." John dried his tears. That was exactly what he needed and wanted. A lion is a strong and mighty animal, the king of the jungle. A lion could conquer and give victory over enemies. Isn't that often what people want in a leader? And a lion of the tribe of Judah reminded John of Israel's greatest king, David, and pointed to a future coming king, a Messiah. That is very good news!

That was what John heard. But when John turned and looked, what he saw was just the opposite of his expectations. "Then I saw between the throne and the four living creatures and among the elders a lamb standing as if it had been slaughtered...." If the lion is at the top of the food chain, the lamb is pretty close to the bottom. A lamb is weak, innocent, and defenseless. In fact, the word for lamb that John uses is a diminutive — lamby or lambkins. And if that weren't enough, this lamb is standing as if it had been slaughtered. It's as if John wants to give us an image bereft of everything we usually associate with a great leader. Who is worthy to open the scroll? Who can bring about God's plan for the redemption of the world? It is *not* the lion, nor any Caesar or Führer — it is the lamb. And all the host of heaven fell before the lamb and broke out into a chorus of passionate praise. "Worthy is the lamb that was slaughtered to receive power and wealth and wisdom and might and honor and glory and blessing!" How does God choose to change the world and bring about its salvation? It is not through power or coercion or the threat of violence. It is not through anything the world understands or values. God changes the world through love and forgiveness. God changes the world through the courageous stand for truth and justice, even if the cost is suffering and death. John described the lamb as having seven horns. A horn was a symbol of power, and seven was a symbol for completeness. Where does complete power lie? It lies in the lamb that was slaughtered. It is what one author calls, "lamb-power." Lamb-power is the wisdom of God that is foolishness to the world, "for God's weakness is stronger than human strength" (1 Corinthians 1:25).

Let me take you back to Germany and give you an example of what I mean. In 1977, I was part of a music group that toured Europe. We flew into West Berlin and crossed into East Berlin at Checkpoint Charlie. When we drove through Leipzig our guide showed us a large building that housed the Stasi, a nickname for the East German Secret Police. They employed thousands of people all intent on spying on their fellow East Germans to control them and force them into obedience. That is the way the world often works, with fear, coercion and threats of violence. That building is today a museum, a monument to the ways the East German government tried to control the population and maintain their power.

Twelve years later, in 1989, the Berlin Wall fell. One of the epicenters for change was the Nikolai Church in Leipzig. While political demonstrations were outlawed, every Monday night at 5:00 the church held a prayer meeting. These prayer meetings became so popular because it was one of the few ways East Germans could meet to express their desire for change. By the summer of 1989 thousands of people were meeting there every week yearning for a change in their lives and their leaders. That yearning came to a head on October 9. Over 70,000 East German citizens gathered around the Nikolai Church. Hundreds of fully armed police and soldiers had been imported to Leipzig. Hospitals were told to prepare for wounded. The pastor of Nikolai Church was Christian Führer. That night those who gathered heard the words of Jesus from the Beatitudes. "Blessed are the poor in spirit for theirs is the kingdom of heaven. Blessed are the meek, for they will inherit the earth. Blessed are those who hunger and thirst for righteousness, for they will be filled. Blessed are the peacemakers, for they will be called children of God." Jesus' words that day were not a call to arms. His was not a call to battle, but a call to non-violence, a call to be peacemakers, a call to love enemies and pray for persecutors. Pastor Führer described what happened next:

More than 2,000 people leaving the church were welcomed by tens of thousands waiting outside with candles in their hands. I will never forget this moment. A person needs two hands to carry a candle: one to hold it and the other to protect the flame — so you can't carry sticks or stones at the same time. The miracle happened. Jesus' spirit of non-violence seized the masses and transformed them into a real and peaceful, powerful presence. Troops and police officers were drawn in and became engaged in conversations. The crowds chanted, "No violence," and the police withdrew.[105]

The Leipzig Communist Security Chief wanted to subdue the rebellion. His police force was well-armed. Soldiers with machine guns stood on top of nearby buildings. But the order to fire was never given. Later on, the security chief admitted, "We planned everything. We were prepared for everything, except for candles and prayers." One month later the wall came down.

How do you change the world? How do you make it a better place? How do you bring about God's reign on the earth? Not with guns and bullets, but with candles and prayers. Not with powerful armies, but with the word of God. Not with a lion, but with a lamb. Der Führer offered Germany a lion, but Pastor Führer offered them the lamb that was slain. This is the wisdom of God that is foolishness to the world, that true and lasting change can only come to the world by a lamb. It is a truth attested to by all the host of heaven, who join before the throne of God, sing a new song to the lamb:

> You are worthy to take the scroll and to open its seals, for you were slaughtered and by your blood you ransomed for God saints from every tribe and language and people and nation; you have made them to be a kingdom and priests serving our God, and they will reign on earth.

Today, Jesus calls us to take up our cross and follow him, or in the words of John, to worship and follow the lamb that was slain.

105 http://godinthegarden.blogspot.com/2009/

It is lamb-power that can truly change our hearts and change our world.

Suggested Prayer of the Day — ELW Easter 3C
Suggested Opening Hymn — "Crown Him with Many Crowns"
Suggested Hymn of the Day — "Blessing, Honor, and Glory"
Suggested Closing Hymn — "Blessing and Honor"

#5 — The Four Horsemen and 9/11: Revelation 6:1-17

If you've watched the news in the past, I'm sure you've been horrified by images coming out of Indonesia. A devastating earthquake toppled buildings to the ground. That was followed by a tsunami that flooded the land. For many in that area this was a total economic collapse. And in the aftermath was the disease and death that followed. It is a reminder how fragile life can be at times and how easily the things we trust in to keep us safe can quickly be taken away.

But that was Indonesia, on the other side of the world. Let's talk about something closer to home. Do you remember where you were several years ago when 9/11 (2001) happened? I arrived at the office of my former church that morning and immediately sensed something was wrong. The secretaries at the church had wheeled a TV into the office. The news reported that a plane that had hit the World Trade Center. We watched horrified as a second plane crashed into the other tower. Shortly after that, a third plane crashed into the Pentagon. A fourth plane crashed into a field in Pennsylvania. No one knew for sure what was going on, but it seemed that our country was under attack. This was a national emergency. Planes everywhere were grounded. Parents rushed to schools to pick up their children. We didn't know what was happening. People were scared. Frantic prayers were spoken for victims and for the rescue workers searching the rubble for survivors. The next evening, we scheduled a prayer service at the church. It was packed. In times of crisis, people naturally turn to God for help. What 9/11 did was to shake us all out of our complacency and our everyday routine. Our sense of safety and security was shattered. We felt vulnerable and afraid. The things we normally trust in were shown to be vulnerable and many of us turned to our faith for reassurance.

Those four planes of 9/11 function much the same way as the four horsemen do in the book of Revelation. We are on a journey through the book of Revelation, and this is the part that where the story starts to get a little scary. The four horsemen of the Apocalypse show up with all their terror. If any of you are *Lord of the Rings* fans, you should remember how you felt every time the Black Riders showed up. If there were a soundtrack to Revelation, the music would definitely start to change, and we would fear that something bad was going to happen. This is when it is important to remember where we have been. In chapters four and five we attended a worship service that was out of this world. We've been taught to see a deeper reality in the universe. We fall before the throne in all-out worship of God and the lamb. The lamb is Jesus Christ, the one "who loves us and freed us from our sins by his blood" (Revelation 1:5). And if things start to get a little scary in our lives, then we need to be reminded to see things from God's perspective. When life gets difficult and trials come our way, then we need to look at them from God's point of view and know that God is there to help see us through our problems.

In chapter five, we saw a scroll with seven seals on it. The scroll represents God's plan for the salvation of the world. The Roman Empire that John lived in had a plan for the world. It was built on an economy maintained by the Roman military. Emperor worship was the glue that held the various parts of the empire together. How do you accomplish the salvation of the world? John had a message for anyone who trusted in Rome's vision for the world. Do you trust in Rome's military? Do you trust in Roman peace to keep the economy flourishing? John reminds his readers that all the things we trust in life to meet our needs and provide us with security can be taken away. Only God's plan will save the world, and the only one who can accomplish that plan is a lamb that was slaughtered.

Now as we read through this chapter we need to remember that this is not a timetable of end-time events, but a description of realities faced by every age. We don't read the book of Revelation so we can know the future; we read it so that we can know God in Jesus.

The first seal is opened and a voice calls out, "Come!" A white horse appears. "Its rider had a bow; a crown was given to him and he came out conquering and to conquer" (Revelation 6:2). In that time horses were valuable tools for war. So having a horse and rider suddenly appear could be a little unsettling and worrisome. Its rider has a bow and he is bent on conquering. Roman citizens hearing this for the first time would have immediately recognized this rider. Rome had enemies on its eastern border that were famous for their cavalry and their ability to ride and shoot a bow at the same time. So John is reminding his readers of a deep seated fear they have of invasion from the east. He is reminding them of the limits of Roman power to protect them. You think that Rome is going to protect you? Think again.

Don't we have similar fears today? I grew up practicing atomic bomb drills in school. We would run into the hall, sit with our faces to the wall and cover our heads (as if that would do any good in a real attack!) What were we afraid of? A nuclear attack from the Russians. It's a bit like the worries we feel today with terrorists trying to infiltrate our country and do us harm. Can we really trust that our country will keep us safe? What do we truly trust in at the deepest level?

If that fear seems a little remote, then the second one hits closer to home. The second seal is broken, and a bright red horse appears. "Its rider was permitted to take peace from the earth so that people would slaughter one another" (Revelation 6:4). Every country in every age yearns for peace. That was one of the gifts the Romans boasted about — the *Pax Romana*. A peaceful empire guaranteed that trade and commerce could flourish. But John warned them not to trust in the peace that Rome gives. That peace can evaporate in an instant.

America has not experienced a war on its own soil since the Civil War. While we haven't known violence in our streets on a widespread scale, we have seen local outbreaks of anarchy. Remember what happened in New Orleans in the aftermath of Katrina? There was a widespread breakdown of law and order. I remember news commentators ask incredulously how this could happen in the United States? What about gang violence? What about school shootings? Do you feel safe to walk the streets of your town at night?

The third horseman hits us right in the pocketbook. "I looked, and there was a black horse! Its rider held a pair of scales in his hand. And I heard a voice …saying, 'A quart of wheat for a day's pay, and three quarts of barley for a day's pay, but do not damage the olive oil and the wine'" (Revelation 6:5-6). There is something wrong with an economy when it takes a whole day's pay just for food. There is no money left for anything else. This black horse represents an economic collapse that affects everyone.

In recent years we have seen way too much of this black horse. I remember nine years ago when the market fell. I saw my pension funds cut in half, and I thought to myself, "There goes my retirement. I'll have to work another five years." And every so often we hear how the Social Security fund will be bankrupt in so many years. What is it you trust in to provide a secure future? The third horseman reminds us that those things can easily be taken away.

And then comes the fourth horse, pale and sickly green. Its name is death. It was "given authority over a fourth of the earth, to kill with sword, famine, and pestilence, and by the wild animals of the earth" (Revelation 6:8). If the third horse affects our economic health, the fourth horse impacts our physical health. No one can escape death, not even Houdini.

The fourth horse reminds us that there is no guarantee in life. We've all known people who died from cancer or for no discernible reason. Every winter we fear the onslaught of a new and virulent flu bug. It was exactly 100 years ago, in 1918, that a flu pandemic killed between 50-100 million people worldwide. It brought the world to its knees. John's use of the fourth horseman is meant to bring us to our knees. What are those things we trust in to provide our basic survival? Those things can be taken away in an instant. John wants us to think clearly and deeply about the foundations of our lives. What is it we trust in?

As the sixth seal was opened a great earthquake took place. "The sun became black as sackcloth, the full moon became like blood, and the stars of the sky fell to the earth… The sky vanished like a scroll rolling itself up, and every mountain and island was removed from its place" (Revelation 6:12-14). John describes a scene of utter destruction. One wonders if John had heard stories of the eruption of Mt. Vesuvius in 79 AD. The city of Pompeii near modern day Naples, Italy, was buried under sixty feet of ash. It was the most luxurious corner of the Roman Empire, a place of power and wealth. Thousands of people died, gone in an instant.

After all this devastation, Revelation chapter 6 ends with a timely question — "Who is able to stand?" Who can survive all this? The answer comes in chapter 7 — "Do not damage the earth or the sea or the trees, until we have marked the servants of our God with a seal on their foreheads" (Revelation 7:3). Who can stand? Those who have been sealed, those who have been claimed by God. We are sealed by the Holy Spirit in the waters of baptism. We are claimed as children of God by the one "who loves us and freed us from our sins by his blood." We are given great and precious promises by God. God "will shelter them. They will hunger no more, and thirst no more; the sun will not strike them, nor any scorching heat; for the lamb at the center of the throne will be their shepherd, and he will guide them to springs of the water of life, and God will wipe away every tear from their eyes" (Revelation 7:16-17).

Who do you trust in? Who do you trust to save you? It's not Caesar, John reminds us. It's not any government or political leader. There is only one who is worthy of our trust. Martin Luther urged us to fear, love, and trust in God above anything else. There is only one foundation that is unshakable, that will withstand any crisis. Trust in God. Follow the lamb.

At the prayer service the day after 9/11, we heard these words from Psalm 46. "God is our refuge and strength, a very present help in trouble. Therefore, we will not fear, though the earth should change, though the mountains shake in the heart of the sea; though its waters roar and foam, though the mountains tremble with its tumult... Be still, and know that I am God... The Lord of hosts is with us; the God of Jacob is our refuge."

Suggested Prayer of the Day — ELW Lectionary 29C
Suggested Opening Hymn — "Blessing and Honor"
Suggested Hymn of the Day — "When Peace Like A River,"
    or "My Lord, What a Mornin'"
Suggested Closing Hymn — "How Firm a Foundation"

#6 — God Has A Plan: Revelation 11:1-15

I was a senior in college the year the first *Star Wars* movie came out. It was amazing how this science fiction fantasy movie captured the imaginations of millions. It was about the conflict between good and evil. Pretty soon we were all saying the words: "May the force be with you!" And we Lutherans would respond, "And also with you!" One of my favorite scenes in the movie is when Darth Vader meets his old teacher, the Jedi Master, Obi-Wan Kenobi. Darth Vader has gone over to the dark side of the force and become a master of evil. After an opening salvo with their light sabers, Darth Vader says to Obi-Wan, "Your powers are weak, old man." Obi-Wan says to him, "You can't win, Darth. You can strike me down, but I shall become more powerful than you can possibly imagine." Obi-Wan is cut down by Darth Vader. And it is Obi-Wan's death that helps lead to a defeat of the empire, something that Darth Vader, with all his power, was not able to foresee.

How can someone's death lead to a victory for good? That is precisely what we are here to celebrate today in our Lord Jesus Christ. His death on the cross was not a defeat, but the ultimate victory in the struggle between good and evil. His death and resurrection are at the very core of our faith as Christians.

We are on this journey through the book of Revelation. Let me review a bit. In chapter five, we saw a scroll with seven seals on it. The scroll represents God's plan for the salvation of the world. Only the lamb who was slaughtered was worthy to open the scroll and break its seals. In chapter six, as the seals were opened, devastations visited the earth. The four horsemen represent basic fears we have about our world — fears of threat from without, fear of violence in our own streets, fear of economic ruin, and the fear of death. These four symbols remind us that all those things we trust in to provide security in our lives can be taken away from us in an instant. We can spend billions on military defense and still not be any more secure than we were before. We can try to lead quiet lives and still be the victim of random violence. We can insure ourselves against economic ruin and still end up losing it all. We can lead healthy lifestyles, exercise and eat the right foods, and still receive a diagnosis of cancer or leukemia from the doctor. Today's news is filled with the sound of hoof beats as these four horsemen gallop their way across the world. And John uses these symbols to remind us that there is only one who can provide us with true security. Put your trust in God alone!

And so what impact do the seals and horses have on humankind? At the end of chapter 6, John tells us that everyone, rich and poor alike, hid from God and refused to worship him. The same thing happened with the next series of woes, symbolized by seven trumpets. John patterned these woes after the Exodus from Egypt story. Just as God used plagues to rescue his people and change Pharaoh's heart, so God used Revelation's trumpets in the same way to rescue his children from an empire built on violence and greed and death. And what was the result? After the sixth trumpet it says that, "The rest of humankind, who were not killed by these plagues, did not repent of the works of their hands or give up worshiping demons and idols of gold and silver and bronze and stone and wood, which cannot see or hear or walk. And they did not repent of their murders or their sorceries or their fornication or their thefts" (9:20-21).

Nothing has worked so far. So what is God going to do? Does God have another plan in mind? Yes. The answer John gives comes in chapters 10 and 11. God calls the church to witness, to testify to the truth of God's love and justice to a world that doesn't want to hear it. God calls the church to witness, even in the face of persecution and death, and to love the world as extravagantly as Christ did. In the New Testament, the word for witness is the same as the word for martyr. Jesus is the faithful witness and calls the church to be witnesses, even if it costs us our lives. When the church does that, the world takes notice, and people come to faith in God.

How does God change the world? How does God redeem the world from its evil and violent ways? It is not through what the world values — power and violence. In John's time, that's how ancient Rome tried to change the world, with the strongest military in history. But John reminds us that God's ways are not our human ways. God changes and heals the world through self-giving sacrificial love. God transforms the world with weakness — with *lamb power*. And the church continues Christ's work through its witness to his love. The early church father Tertullian wrote that the blood of the martyrs is the seed of the church. He wrote that because he had seen it with his own eyes. Tertullian had converted to Christianity based in part on his wonder at Christians' faithfulness in the face of martyrdom, and it clearly had a similar effect on others as well. The early church grew until in the fourth century, it became the official religion of the Roman Empire.

I could give you example after example of Christians who remained faithful in the face of death. Justin Martyr was a leader in the early Christian church. He was arrested and told to renounce his faith. Justin refused and was beheaded. Or people like Perpetua, who converted to Christianity at a time of great persecution. She was arrested and brought before the governor to deny her faith and perform the sacrifice to the emperor. She refused, and Perpetua and her friends were brought to the arena where they were attacked by gladiators and wild animals and killed. To be a martyr is to be a witness, and the witness of these martyrs to their faith in Jesus Christ had a power that the Romans could not understand. And eventually, Christianity became the official religion of the Roman Empire.

Brian Blount has written a book about Revelation from the African American perspective. He tells about how Martin Luther King Jr. led a movement to change racial injustice in our country by speaking truth to power. This truth-telling grew out of the faith of Christians who were inspired by the non-violence of Jesus. When the world watched as Christians were the victims of horrible violence and injustice, there was moral outrage. Real change came to our country in the form of civil rights legislation. Brian wrote, "One can say that the civil rights protesters who were beaten, water hosed, bombed, threatened, tortured, and even killed were, like the lamb, slaughtered. But one would not properly call them victims, even if their victory did come at what were often tragic costs. At the very moment their oppressors executed their violence against them, the moment of their symbolic slaughter, their battle was won." That is the power of witness. That is lamb power.

In 2015, the world was horrified at the death of twenty Coptic Christian martyrs. They were captured by ISIS and beheaded for their faith. At the moment of their death, they all cried out the name of Jesus. It was a powerful testimony to their faith. And while the Coptic Church community in Egypt grieved, they also celebrated the faith of these martyrs.

How is God going to change the world? God will change it through you and me and our loving witness to Christ's love and justice to bring change to the world. The powers of darkness will oppose us. But our mission is to speak truth to power and to bring light to the darkness. That is our mission given us in baptism. We are joined to one another in "God's mission for the life of the world." Our mission is not to fight evil with evil, but to fight evil with good. We aren't called to take up arms, but called to follow the lamb that was slain, to oppose evil with lamb power. We walk in the light. We speak truth. We love extravagantly, and we forgive without end. These are the gifts we have been given in Jesus Christ. This is the mission that God sends us to share with the world, even at the cost of our lives.

The two witnesses made a difference and so can you and I. At the end of chapter 11, everyone gave glory to God, the seventh trumpet was blown, and the heavens broke out into song. "The kingdom of the world has become the kingdom of our Lord and of his [Christ], and he will reign forever and ever." This is a song that George Frederic Handel made famous in the "Hallelujah Chorus" from his oratorio, Messiah. The words come right out of the book of Revelation. When Handel completed the "Hallelujah Chorus", he reportedly told his servant, "I did think I did see all heaven before me, and the great God himself seated on his throne, with his company of angels." Let's listen to a part of the chorus now.

Suggested Prayer of the Day — ELW p. 59 Martyrs
Suggested Opening Hymn — "Lift High the Cross"
Suggested Hymn of the Day — "Faith of Our Fathers"
Suggested Closing Hymn — "Rise, Shine, You People"

#7 — Evil is Exposed: Revelation 12:13 — 13:18

We have been on this journey through the book of Revelation, and today we come to one of the scariest parts of the book with the mark of the beast. People may not know much about the book of Revelation, but this is one symbol that seems to have worked its way into popular culture. Most everyone seems to know the number 666. Twelve years ago, the movie called, *The Omen*, was released on the sixth day of the sixth month of the sixth year of the new millennium.

The Omen was a remake of the 1976 classic film about a young boy named Damien, who was discovered to bear the mark of the beast in his scalp. His family was unaware that Damien was destined to become the antichrist and lead the world to the events of Armageddon.

In typical fashion, Hollywood has co-opted religious themes and twisted them for commercial purposes. Unfortunately, what people know about the 'mark of the beast' is largely what they learn from pop culture or from those end-time predictors who misinterpret Revelation. And, since this is probably the last passage in the Bible that many of us pastors would ever choose to preach on, there is often no one to set the record straight. No wonder people are afraid to read Revelation! When we actually read the book, we find that there are two groups marked on the forehead — those who follow the beast and those who follow the lamb. Why don't we ever hear about the followers of the lamb in the movies? Both are marked on the forehead with a name. Those who follow the beast are marked with the number of its name — 666. Those who follow the lamb are marked on the forehead with his name. And the book of Revelation is very clear who the lamb is — the risen Lord Jesus Christ. Revelation is also clear who the beast is — the Roman Empire that demanded worship of its subjects and threatened death for those who refused to cooperate. The mark on the forehead symbolizes our values and priorities in life. And the question Revelation asked its first readers was this: whose name is on your forehead? Who do you follow, the beast or the lamb?

Over the years there's been a lot of speculation about the symbol 666, much of it just plain wrong. Most scholars think that 666 is a form of alphabetical code where letters of the alphabet are assigned a numerical value. Add them up and you have the number of someone's name. And that name is Caesar Nero. Before his death in 68 AD, Nero captured Christians and rolled them in pitch, then hung them on poles, and lit them on fire to light the Coliseum at night. Other Christians were sown into animal skins to be torn apart by wild dogs. No wonder John describes Nero as a beast. It's a revolting image meant to give us insight into the true nature of the Roman Empire and its idolatrous claims.

But there is another way we could look at this number — 666. Numbers function as symbols in the book of Revelation. Six is the number for humankind. Human beings were created on the sixth day. The number seven is perhaps the most significant number in Revelation. Seven is the number for completeness or perfection. Therefore, six is not quite complete, not quite perfect, one short of seven. We human beings always fall short, don't we? That's what the six represents. And when you have three of them, which is the number for God, you have a symbol that represents the human attempt to be God. 666 is Adam and Eve reaching for the apple because they wanted to be like God. 666 represents the claims of any institution or government for the ultimate allegiance and obedience that only God deserves.

Our reading today starts a new section in Revelation. And John wants to give his churches an answer to the questions — Where does evil come from? Why are Christians being persecuted? John gives us an answer. The evil we experience in the world, whether from individuals or institutions or governments, comes ultimately from Satan. Satan lost a battle in heaven and now is making trouble on earth accusing Christians before God. In chapter 13, Satan is joined by two beasts, one from the sea and one from the land. The beast from the sea is Rome and its armies which literally came across the sea to conquer and impose its will on nations. It used violence and threat to control and dominate. The beast from the land represents those local officials who wanted to promote Roman culture and power to curry favor with Roman officials. Together these three represent an "unholy trinity" that John wanted to expose as counterfeit. Instead of Christians buying into the Roman propaganda that they were the saviors of the world bringing peace to the nations, John wanted Christians to know that was a lie. John wanted them to know a deeper reality, that peace comes only through Jesus Christ.

Most of you have seen the movie, *The Wizard of Oz*. There is a scene at the end of the movie when Dorothy and the others finally get in to see the wizard and ask him to keep his promises to them. They were intimidated and frightened by the smoke and lights and the powerful voice, cowering in fear, duped into believing whatever the wizard told them. That was what the wizard wanted them to believe. It was Dorothy's little dog, Toto, who pulled back the curtain to reveal the true nature of things. The great and powerful wizard was a fake, a phony, just an old man pulling levers who had no power to do anything. In a way, that is what John is doing with the image of the beast, pulling back the curtain and showing Christians the true nature of the society they lived in. He was telling them that Rome was not worthy of their worship, their allegiance and love. Rome was built on a foundation of violence and injustice. The Roman peace came only at the end of a sword, and that peace was kept only at the threat of death. It was a peace that benefitted the powerful and the wealthy.

So who is the beast today? One scholar has said that the church in every age must name the beast, must speak out against those things in our world that are beast-like. The beast isn't necessarily any one individual. The beast is any government or movement that claims the ultimate loyalty that should only be given to God. The beast is anything that asks us to sacrifice our values in order to follow it. The beast will ask us to live a lie. The beast cannot stand the light of truth and will persecute those who are the truthtellers and whistleblowers in society. The beast will stand up and boast of its accomplishments and demand that we bow down and worship at its altar.

Let me give you a few examples. In Germany, in 1934, a group of Christians gathered in Germany to oppose the Nazi party and the growing influence that they had over the Christian church. They issued a declaration saying that the movement Hitler had started was antithetical to the Gospel of Jesus Christ. They pulled back the curtain to try to show German Christians that they were following the beast. They tried to convince the Germans not to be seduced by the Nazi movement. Hitler promised to improve their lives and make Germany great again. But Hitler's movement was built on lies and violence.

The same thing happened in the 1980s when church after church issued condemnations of the South African Apartheid government, saying that it was established on lies that were contrary to the gospel. God has created all people and all races, and God loves them all equally. Again, the church was pulling back the curtain to expose the beast-like lies of the South African government.

Are there beast-like elements in our world today? If John were here today, what curtains would he want us to peek behind, what lies to expose? Are there governments or movements that want to buy your soul and get you to live a lie — especially the lies they want to promote? Are there movements that tempt us to sacrifice our values and compromise our faith as followers of Christ? It amazes me when I see some Christians in our country today so quickly leave behind their values in order to gain political power. The bottom line for Christians is not what leader or political party is going to make us richer. The bottom line for Christians is following Jesus Christ, the lamb that was slain, and living out Jesus' values in our world today.

One of the values enshrined in our country today is that of a free press. It's really the idea that the government should not control the information we receive, but that the press should be free to report the truth, even if that truth is critical of the government. But that can be dangerous in governments run by dictators. Just look at what happened to Jamal Kashoggi, who was trying to tell the truth about the Saudi government. When governments seek to control the press, then news easily becomes propaganda, lies they want you to believe. And then governments become beast-like, demanding our worship or threatening death.

The beast dresses in many disguises today. It wins every time we lose our prophetic witness to the truth and compromise our faith. The beast wins every time we grow complacent or afraid to speak out. The book of Revelation is a call to Christians of every age to reject the idolatrous claims of the beast in whatever contemporary form they appear. The book of Revelation is a call to worship God alone, and to conquer through our faithful witness to Jesus, the lamb who was slaughtered.

As we Christians participate in our society as responsible citizens, we do so as followers of Jesus Christ. We love and serve our country, but our ultimate allegiance is to Jesus Christ. The values that we live by are Jesus' values. And when we see individuals or governments behaving like a beast, we must say "no!' and follow Jesus, the lamb who was slain, even if it comes with a cost.

Jesus Christ is the true source of life, of love and joy and peace. Follow him alone.

Suggested Prayer of the Day — ELW Renewers of Society #2
Suggested Opening Hymn — "A Mighty Fortress is Our God"
Suggested Hymn of the Day — "God of Grace and God of
Glory"
Suggested Closing Hymn — "Canticle of the Turning"

#8 — Whose Side Are You On? Revelation 14

In 1521, Martin Luther stood before the emperor and representatives of the Pope. All the powers of church and state were brought to bear on this German priest. They demanded that he recant his teachings of the Bible, which they saw as a threat to their power. If Luther refused, he would almost certainly face martyrdom. If he gave in to their demands, it would bring an end to the Reformation and show that Luther didn't really believe what he had written. In an epic showdown, Luther said this: "Unless I am convinced by scripture and plain reason — I do not accept the authority of the popes and councils, for they have contradicted each other — my conscience is captive to the word of God. I cannot and I will not recant anything for to go against conscience is neither right nor safe. God help me. Amen." Martin Luther in that moment needed to pick a side, and he chose to follow his conscience and to follow Christ. For that he was excommunicated from the church. The emperor had promised him safe passage back to his home, but after that, anyone could kill Luther without penalty. Luther fully expected to be killed for his faith, but the prince of the area where he lived decided to protect him. The Reformation continued, and the rest is history.

The Christians in Revelation faced a similar situation to Luther. John spelled it out for them. There are followers of the beast, and there are followers of the lamb. Christians must pick a side, because they couldn't do both. Who will you choose to follow? And John wanted to make it easier for Christians to choose sides by showing them the end of the Roman Empire.

I love this autumn season of the year. Finally, we've had some decent weather so that the farmers could get in the field to harvest their crops. The corn and soybean fields are ripe. Farmers who planted corn seed last spring expect to harvest corn. Farmers who planted soybeans last spring expect to harvest soybeans. It is a principle the Bible is clear about. You reap what you sow. If you sow love and kindness, you will reap love and kindness in return. If you sow hatred and violence, you will reap hatred and violence.

John shows us that in the end time, two groups of people are harvested. The first are those who follow the Lord. "Blessed are the dead who from now on die in the Lord.' 'Yes,' says the Spirit, 'they will rest from their labors, for their deeds follow them.'" The second group that is harvested are those who follow the beast. In describing them, the harvest images are bloody and gruesome. Blood as high as a horse's bridle for 200 miles. God's wrath being poured out on the earth.

How are we to understand these images? Again, we don't read these images literally. John doesn't mean what he says. John means what he means. These symbols are meant to have an emotional impact on us. The people reading this for the first time would see the end of the Roman Empire in such vivid terms that they would reject Rome and choose the lamb.

But there is another way to understand these symbols. John patterns many of these tragedies after the plagues that God sent to Egypt to rescue God's people. God's wrath or God's anger serves a greater purpose. Just like the exodus from Egypt, God wants to free God's people from persecution and oppression. God's desire is not to punish but to restore.

Think of God's wrath like tough love. Have you ever known someone caught up in an addiction? They make terrible choices. Often, they will choose their addiction over a marriage or over family. They can lose everything. You can get them into treatment, and sometimes it will work, but other times they just go back to their addiction. Sometimes the only option is tough love, to let that person suffer the consequences of their choices until life gets so bad they come to their senses. I think of God's wrath that way, as tough love. And when we cry out to God out of our pain, God comes to our rescue. God's desire is not to punish, but to restore.

God wants to restore all people to himself, and sometimes that requires tough love.

The year was 1861. The Civil War had just started and there had been a few battles. People began to realize that this war was not going to be over soon, and increasing numbers of men were being conscripted to fight in the war. Julia Ward Howe lived in Washington, DC and witnessed as troops arrived singing their war songs. One evening she woke up early with the words to a song going through her mind. She wrote down the words. The song became one of the most popular during the war. We know it today as the "Battle Hymn of the Republic". Some of the words in the song come directly from Revelation 14.

> Mine eyes have seen the glory of the coming of the Lord;
> He is trampling out the vintage where the grapes of wrath are stored;
> He hath loosed the fateful lightning of His terrible swift sword:
> His truth is marching on.

Julia Ward Howe saw directly that America was paying a price for its sin of slavery. It was reaping what it had sown. The price in the lives of men killed and blood spilt was horrific. Maybe not blood as high as a horse's bridle for 200 miles, but close. The last verse is a direct reference to the end of slavery.

> In the beauty of the lilies Christ was born across the sea,
> With a glory in his bosom that transfigures you and me.
> As he died to make men holy, let us live to make men free,
> While God is marching on.

God's wrath was poured out on our country in a way we had never seen before. We were addicted to the institution of slavery, an institution built on lies and violence and injustice. The only thing that was going to free us from our addiction was war. Don't think of it as God punishing us. Our sin of slavery was its own punishment. And God used that punishment to free us from our addiction to slavery.

We are still paying the price for our racism 150 years later. Hate crimes like yesterday's shooting in Pittsburgh show that we still have a struggle to root out racism in our society. Movements like the #MeToo movement or Black Lives Matter show that we still struggle with inequality and injustice. John reminds us that we must pick a side.

Revelation 14 begins with this verse: "Then I looked, and there was the lamb, standing on Mount Zion! And with him were one hundred and forty-four thousand who had his name and his Father's name written on their foreheads." It is a mighty army following after the lamb. But the weapons of this army are not guns and bullets. This army uses lamb power, the power of the lamb's sacrificial self-giving love. Lamb power is the power of non-violent resistance. Lamb power is courage in opposition to injustice. It is the power of forgiveness to bring healing.

And did you notice that these followers of the lamb were marked on the forehead, just as the followers of the beast were. God's name is written on their forehead. You and I, too, are part of that army who follow the lamb. God's name is marked on our foreheads in the waters of baptism. We bear that mark with us throughout life and into the life to come. When we are baptized, we are asked three questions, or our parents are asked those questions for us if we are too young. "Do you renounce the devil and all the forces that defy God? Do you renounce the powers of this world that rebel against God? Do you renounce the ways of sin that draw you from God?" To each question, the response is: I renounce them! We are asked to choose sides. We are invited to reject the beast and follow the lamb.

Baptism is what joins us to God's "mission for the life of the world." We are called to follow the lamb and reject the ways of the beast. We follow Jesus Christ and devote our lives to sharing God's love with the world. Are there beast-like elements in your life today, in your home or school, in your workplace or community? Let us recommit to speaking truth and sharing God's love, the unconditional love and grace God has so graciously given us in

Jesus Christ.

Suggested Prayer of the Day — Reformation Day #1
Suggested Opening Hymn — "A Mighty Fortress Is Our God"
Suggested Hymn of the Day — "Let Us Ever Walk With Jesus"
Suggested Closing Hymn — "Mine Eyes Have Seen the Glory"

#9 — When Evil Self-Destructs: Revelation 17

It was just one week ago that the nation was gripped with lottery fever. It was the largest jackpot in history — $1.6 billion. I'll admit it — We bought two tickets. There's probably some entertainment value from playing. It is fun to fantasize what you would do with all that money. There are all kinds of get-rich-quick schemes. Some of them like the lottery are legal. But what if someone approached you with a scheme to make some easy money, but you had to do something that you suspected wasn't quite right or maybe against the law? What would you choose? On the one hand, wouldn't it be nice to get out of debt and not have to worry about your financial future? On the other hand, would you be willing to sell your soul to get there?

I say this because that's the kind of dilemma we are presented in our reading today. We've been on this journey through Revelation and we've encountered all kinds of bizarre images and symbols. Some of those symbols are hard to understand. And some of those symbols are just hard to stomach. The image we have today is one of those symbols that is revolting and disgusting to our modern sensitivities. John presents us with two major symbols to understand the Roman Empire he was living in. A few weeks ago, we talked about the beast with seven heads. The beast conquers and imposes its will on countries with violence and uses fear and threats to enforce loyalty. Today we have the second image John uses to describe the Roman empire. He calls it a whore, a prostitute who seduces the world with promises of wealth and pleasure.

I want you to think of these two images like the carrot and the stick. The beast represents the stick and the whore represents the carrot. If the stick won't get you to worship Caesar, the carrot might seduce you into it. Why not deny your faith and participate in the Roman economy? Get rich. Celebrate Rome and all things Roman. Worship their gods and goddesses.

Let me tell you about one of those goddesses. Her name was Roma and she was the patron goddess of Rome. Her image was everywhere. She sat on a shield and wore a helmet and held a scepter. She was portrayed as victorious, strong and proud. She was the divine protector of Rome. But the prophet John didn't see her that way. He used language that showed what he really thought of *Roma*. He called her a whore.

Here is another way to think of this. When you see the Statue of Liberty, you immediately know that symbol represents the United States. You also associate Lady Liberty with a certain set of values like purity and compassion, hospitality and welcome, refuge and shelter to the persecuted and the impoverished. But what if someone showed a picture of Lady Liberty dressed in a bikini with a boa around her neck, a cigarette on her lips, and instead holding a torch, she was holding a martini glass? It would be offensive to us. We call that a lampoon. The artist would be sending a message that Lady Liberty stands for a different set of values. That is the sort of thing John was doing here with the Roman goddess Roma. John portrayed her in the most vulgar and degrading terms. He was sending a message counter to the propaganda of the Roman Empire. He was revealing the truth about the Roman Empire and its values.

Let me tell you another story that illustrates this. In 2004, the people of Ukraine were electing a new president. Viktor Yushchenko was running as a challenger to the ruling party. He was comfortably ahead in the polls, but on the day of the election the ruling party tampered with the voting results. The official news source came on the evening broadcast to announce the result. "Ladies and gentlemen, we announce that the challenger, Victor Yuschchenko has been decisively defeated." In the lower right-hand corner of the TV screen was a smaller box with a young woman who was an interpreter for the deaf. Her name was Natalia Dmitruk. As the news reporter read the lies of the regime, Natalia Dmitruk refused to translate that. Instead, she signed another message. "I'm addressing all the deaf citizens of Ukraine. They are lying and I'm ashamed to translate those lies. Yushchenko is our president." The deaf community mobilized. Word began to spread. A protest was organized and after a few weeks, they forced a new election, and Viktor Yushchenko became president.

It seems to me that this is exactly what the prophet John was doing. He is like that sign interpreter in the little box telling the truth, revealing what was really going on. In spite of a huge propaganda machine by the Roman empire, John was revealing that Rome was nothing but a drunken seducer whose end would come quickly.

John is actually standing in a long tradition of the ancient Hebrew prophets. They often used sexual immorality as a metaphor or symbol to describe God's unfaithful people. It wasn't about sex. It was about idolatry and chasing after other gods. It was about their lack of faithfulness and trust in God. For John, Rome was either a beast who threatened Christians with violence, or Rome was a seducer who used the promise of luxury and wealth to entice Christians away from their faith in Christ. Would you sell your soul and turn your back on Jesus in order to get ahead, to be rich and prosperous? These were some of the choices that were facing ancient Christians. They are the same choices we Christians face today. There is nothing wrong in being rich, but it is how we get rich that makes all the difference in the world. If we have to compromise our faith in Christ and our values in order to become wealthy, then it isn't worth it. John wants us to think deeply about the world we live in. Reject the beasts. Reject the seducers. Follow the lamb. Trust in Jesus Christ. Jesus has conquered.

John made a prediction about the Roman Empire. He showed Christians the natural end of this violent and degraded empire. It is a disgusting picture he paints. "And the ten horns that you saw are ten kings they and the beast will hate the whore; they will make her desolate and naked; they will devour her flesh and burn her up with fire." The picture is ugly and revolting.

John intends it to be that way to make Christians turn away from Rome and turn to Christ. What John is trying to show us here is that any empire, any nation or institution that is built on lies and fear, on violence and injustice, has within it the seeds of its own destruction. It will eventually reap what it has sown. Its people will hate the inequality and injustice and they will rise up to overthrow it.

We could say the same thing about a family. Parents, do your kids obey you because they fear you, or because they love you? Maybe it's a mixture of both. But a family based on fear and violence has within it the seeds of its own destruction. We could say the same about a workplace. Do you give your employers your best effort because you fear them, or because you love and respect them? Some of us have had some horrible bosses and we stay in a job because we need the income. But now let's talk about God. Do you believe in God because you're afraid if you don't you will spend eternity in hell? Or do you believe in God because your heart has been captured by God's unconditional love for you and the grace given you in Jesus Christ? That's why I follow the lamb. That's why I come to worship every week, to be reminded that God loves me and that my sins are forgiven. That good news has the power to change our hearts.

John has a message for us today. Build your family on a foundation of love and respect. Build your community on a foundation of justice and fairness and compassion for the poor and needy. When people are loyal out of love and not out of fear, that is a strong bond that will not be broken. When we build on a foundation of love, then we are following the lamb. We are using lamb power. That is especially true when we speak truth to the beasts of our world and meet their hatred with non-violence, with sacrificial love and forgiveness. We need to reject the beasts and bullies of our world. We need to reject the seducers of our world who try to get us to sell our souls with promises of making us rich.

John has a word of hope. If you are in a difficult place in your life, if you are going through challenging times, don't give up.

Maybe it seems like you are facing a beast in your life. Don't give up. Maybe it seems like you are being strongly tempted to cut corners or cheat just to get ahead. Don't give in. John's message to you is that the lamb has conquered. Jesus has conquered. Love is stronger than violence. Kindness is stronger than hatred. Follow the lamb that was slain. That word is as relevant today as it was 2,000 years ago.

Suggested Prayer of the Day — ELW Lent 1A
Suggested Opening Hymn — "Jesus Shall Reign"
Suggested Hymn of the Day — "When Pain of the World Surrounds Us"
Suggested Closing Hymn — "O Jesus, I Have Promised"

#10 — A Picture Gallery of the End: Revelation 19-20

It was exactly 100 years ago that World War One ended. On November 11, 1918, an armistice was signed bringing an end to the hostilities between the Allies and Germany. World War One was described as the "war to end all wars." An estimated nine million soldiers and seven million civilians died as a direct result of the war. (That would be like the entire population of Minnesota, Wisconsin, Iowa, North and South Dakota combined.) The war also contributed to the 1918 influenza epidemic, which contributed to deaths of between 50-100 million people worldwide. Can you imagine what that must have been like, the scale of the devastation and death worldwide? For our ancestors living through those events, it must have seemed like the end of the world. I wonder if they thought they were living in end-times? Did they use words like apocalyptic or Armageddon to describe their world? Did they think that Jesus return was imminent? The world had never seen death and destruction before on this scale.

Armageddon! We use that word a lot in our culture to describe events that could lead to the destruction of the world. Hollywood even makes movies about it. Let me tell you about Armageddon. In the fall of 2011, I had the opportunity to tour Israel. One of the places we visited was Tel Megiddo. It is a national park in Israel today. Lots of tourists visit this place. It is the site of many famous battles in the ancient world. Megiddo is basically a hill that was strategically located at the crossroads of two ancient highways. King Solomon had a fortress built here with stables for hundreds of horses. But Megiddo is most famous as the site described in the book of Revelation for a final battle between the forces of good and evil. Another word for a hill is Har. Har-Megiddo or Armageddon. We were there in November and walked up the hill to the top to see the ruins. It was an impressive view of the surrounding valley. But as we were there, a most unusual thing happened. A storm cloud moved in and it started to rain. It was a brief rain, just five minutes. Our tour guide said it almost never rains in November. But as we looked out over the valley, a rainbow appeared stretching from end to end. I thought of God's promise to Noah that the rainbow would be a sign that God would never destroy the earth again. How ironic to see a rainbow in the place where the end of the world is supposed to happen — Armageddon. Maybe Armageddon isn't the end of the world after all. Maybe the prophet John who wrote the book of Revelation wants us to see something else in this symbol.

I've said it before. When we read the book of Revelation it's important to remember that the prophet John doesn't mean what he says; he means what he means. He doesn't want us to read this literally. Armageddon isn't a place you can point to on a map. It is a symbol of the ongoing struggle between good and evil. And it is a symbol that someday God will defeat evil.

That is a word of hope to all who yearn for peace. It feels overwhelming to hear almost daily of yet another mass shooting. In 2018 so far, we have had 307 mass shootings in 311 days. When will it end? We grow tired and weary of working for peace and justice in our world. We think that we have made great strides in our country on equality. And then a shooting happens like last week in Pittsburgh happens and we see an increase in anti-Semitism, a reminder of the ongoing struggle to end racism in our country. These are just a few of the things that discourage us and make us wonder if it will ever end. The symbol of Armageddon is meant to give us hope that one day, God will indeed bring an end to evil. Mourning, crying, and pain will be no more, and God will wipe every tear from our eyes.

Armageddon is just one of many symbols that John shows us near the end of his book. It's like a picture gallery, and each picture has a message to bring us. The rider on the white horse is Jesus coming with his army, but this army has no weapons. There is only a sword coming from Jesus' mouth. Again, the sword is a symbol of the word of God, God's truth that sets us free. Jesus' army is unlike any other. Their only weapons are the word of God. We don't fight this battle with guns and bullets. We fight it with God's word, with truth, love, forgiveness, and the non-violent stand against injustice with the power of the lamb that was slain. It's like the quote from Martin Luther King Jr. "Darkness cannot drive out darkness; only light can. Hatred cannot drive out hatred; only love can."

There is another picture that John gives us, and that is of the millennium, a thousand-year period of peace. And at the end of that period, Satan will be released again for a final battle and his final destruction. Again, we need to ask what John is trying to tell us with this symbol. We thought that World War One was the war to end all wars. That idea was based on a naïve view of human nature. We know that just 22 years later, World War Two started. And following that the Korean War, then the Vietnam War, and now the Afghanistan war. Evil keeps popping up its head. After a period of peace, after the world catches its breath from the last war, another war breaks out. Perhaps John wants us to know that instead of this endless cycle of violence and war, there will come a time when God will bring an end to war and killing and hatred.

There is one more picture that John gives us, and we need to talk about it. Minnesota is called the land of 10,000 lakes. Minnesotans dream of having a lake cabin. There is a popular saying, "Life is better at the lake." But John talks about a lake that no one wants to visit — the Lake of Fire. It is a place of judgment and punishment and one of the most horrifying images in the whole of the Bible. Western art and literature is filled with depictions of the lake of fire and those being burned in it. Preachers have found the lake of fire to be a powerful tool to manipulate people with fear. Hellfire and brimstone!

In 35 years of preaching, I don't ever remember preaching a sermon about hell until now. One of the most interesting Bible studies I have ever led was a Bible study on hell. I called it, "Go to Hell with Pastor Rolf." You see, when we talk about hell, we are really talking about God and the kind of God we worship. If hell is a place of eternal torment and torture, how do we reconcile that with a God of love who has revealed himself in Jesus' death and resurrection? So again, when we talk about hell and the Lake of Fire, we need to remember to interpret this symbol the same way we interpret the other symbols John gives us. The Lake of Fire is described as the place of second death. It is the ultimate destination of evil. If the symbol of the millennium reminds us that evil can resurrect its ugly head at any time, the lake of fire is there to reassure us that evil will ultimately be destroyed, never to come back again.

It's interesting that in our Apostle's Creed, our ancient confession of faith, it doesn't talk about hell. Jesus descends to the dead. It was a way of saying that he really died and wasn't resuscitated. It does, however, tell us that Jesus will come again "to judge the living and the dead." There will be a judgment, that is for sure. The good news we proclaim is that our sins have already been judged in the cross of Christ.

There is evil in the world. But it's not just out there. The axis of evil runs straight through our hearts. I know it does through mine. I am profoundly aware of my sins and shortcomings. It is only by the grace of God that I can make it into heaven. But I used to wonder that when I arrived in heaven, how long it would take before I messed up and did something wrong. Then what would happen? Would I get kicked out of heaven? Would I get a divine "time-out" to suffer for a while before I could get back in?

I want to tell you today that there is good news in the Lake of Fire. The evil in the world, including the evil that lurks in our own hearts, will all be burned up in the lake of fire. God's purpose in the world is not to punish sin. Sin is its own punishment. God's purpose is to rescue us from sin. God's purpose is to free us from sin's grip on our lives and to restore our relationship with God. That happens in the Lake of Fire. It is a fire that refines and purifies.

These can be frightening symbols from the book of Revelation. But when we understand how John uses them, we can find comfort and hope. If you are feeling tired and weary of this old world, if you are tempted to give up, just remember that God has already won a victory in Jesus' death and resurrection. And one day that victory will be made complete when God makes all things new.

Suggested Prayer of the Day — ELW Lectionary 22B
Suggested Opening Hymn — "I Know that My Redeemer Lives"
Suggested Hymn of the Day — "How Firm a Foundation"
Suggested Closing Hymn — "Come, Ye Thankful People Come"

#11 — When God Comes Down: Revelation 19:6-9; 21:1-18

How many of you have watched the news this week and seen the horrifying images from northern California of the wildfire's destruction? Every day the list of missing increases and the death toll climbs. The town of Paradise, California, has burned to the ground. I remember watching one survivor being interviewed. Through her tears she said that Paradise was gone. It struck me as ironic as we gather here today to read this passage from Revelation about paradise. The city of Paradise may be gone, but the paradise promised by God is as alive as ever.

We often think of Paradise as a place we go to when we die. And it certainly is that. The apostle Paul said that when he died, he would be with the Lord. Jesus said that he was going to prepare a place for us and that we would be with him. But John has a different focus here. John's focus is on this world. We don't go up to heaven. Heaven comes down to this world. Heaven comes down and makes this old world new. "And I saw the holy city, the New Jerusalem, coming down out of heaven from God, prepared as a bride adorned for her husband. And I heard a loud voice from the throne saying, 'See, the home of God is among mortals. He will dwell with them as their God; they will be his peoples, and God himself will be with them.'" God comes down to dwell with humankind on earth. That is the gospel, the good news that God has come down to us in Jesus Christ. "And the word became flesh and lived (dwelt) among us" (John 1:14). God has come down to us in Jesus Christ to free us and rescue us from our sins. That's what grace is. God comes down to us. God always comes down. That is so different from much of religion where we think we have to climb up to God by our good deeds or by behaving the way God wants us to. We don't go up to God; God comes down to us, in the midst of our pain and brokenness, in the midst of the mess we have made of our lives and world. God comes down to us announcing forgiveness of sins through Jesus Christ. That is grace, something we don't deserve or earn, but something God gives us in Christ because God so loved the world. God comes down and makes this old world new. And that is what John wants us to know. Paradise isn't some pie in the sky by and by. Paradise is a city of God that comes down to this earth and makes it new.

The other day I was driving out in the country and saw a sign in someone's farmyard that said, "Welcome to Jim's little slice of heaven." I'm not sure what Jim means by that sign, but here's what I think it means. On a farm you see the power of nature. You are surrounded by things that grow, crops and animals. You watch the sunrise and sunset each day. You notice the weather patterns change, and mark time as the seasons change. God has placed a power in nature and in that power we sense God's presence and blessing. But there's more. That little slice of heaven is a place where we belong, a place we call home. It is a place where we feel loved and we feel safe, protected from things that would harm us. I think of all that when I think of that little slice of heaven here on earth. That is what God wants us to experience now in this life, on this earth God has given us.

But there's something else John wants us to know about heaven. John describes heaven as a city. There may be a garden in the midst of it, but heaven is a city. It is a place where people live together, where they get along with each other, where they love and care for each other. Heaven is not just "me and Jesus walking together in the garden." Heaven is me and Jesus and a whole bunch of other people. It is a city where we experience God's presence and blessing in community with others. Heaven is a place where people love and respect each other, even when they disagree.

Sometimes when you hear people talking about Bible prophecy, they talk about the destruction of the earth in a final battle. But that is not the image we are given in Revelation. There is a saying: 'We don't know the future, but we know the one who holds the future.' That is the message of Revelation. Whatever happens in the future, we know that God will be there. And instead of an apocalyptic end of the world, God comes down to renew the world. John reminds us that "the one who was seated on the throne said, 'See, I am making all things new.'" God did not say, "I am making all new things." God is not going to destroy everything and start over again. God did that once with Noah and promised never to do it again. No, God is making all things new. God is going to take this old, broken world and renew it. "And God himself will be with them; he will wipe every tear from their eyes. Death will be no more; mourning and crying and pain will be no more, for the first things have passed away."

We have heard a lot about the caravan of refugees coming up through Mexico, people fleeing the violence in their homelands, in search of a new home, a safe place to live and raise their families. Some of them describe horrifying stories of gang violence, of rape, torture or extortion. Can you blame them for wanting a better life? Isn't that what we all want? In John's vision, God promises that heaven will be a place of safety, free from violence, fear, and oppression. "But as for the cowardly, the faithless, the polluted, the murderers, the fornicators, the sorcerers, the idolaters, and all liars, their place will be in the lake that burns with fire and sulfur, which is the second death." Have you ever had your house broken into? You feel violated and unsafe. That will not happen in this new city. John reassures us that everyone will be safe there.

There is one more thing John tells us about this new community God is creating. One of the most common images used in the Bible to portray heaven is that of a marriage feast. Jesus' first miracle was turning water into wine at a wedding feast. In a wedding feast, there is joy and celebration. That is a sign of God's presence. This past summer we experienced a very special wedding feast when my daughter married a man whose mother came from Nigeria. Daughter Siri got married to wonderful man named Allen. Allen is black and his mother came from Nigeria. The wedding of a firstborn son is a big deal in that Nigerian culture, and this mother wanted a traditional Nigerian ceremony to which she could invite all her friends, the whole community. So, there were actually two weddings, the one the kids planned themselves, and the next day a traditional Nigerian ceremony that the mother planned. The costumes were beautiful and colorful. The music was loud and there was much dancing and joyous celebration. When the bride and groom came in with their attendants, they danced. There was a money shower where people threw dollar bills at them as they danced, a symbolic prayer for prosperity and blessing in their home. And there was food and drink, lots of it to celebrate with. That, John said, is what heaven is like. It is the marriage supper of the lamb, Jesus. And the bride is the church, the people Jesus has redeemed. God will make a home with us and fill our hearts with joy and peace. There will be feasting and celebration when God comes down.

God is not going to destroy this world in some Armageddon style battle. God comes down to this world to renew it. And that is not just in some distant future. God comes down to us today. God comes down to us as we follow the lamb and rely on lamb power to change our world. God comes down to us whenever the good news is proclaimed. God comes down in the waters of baptism. God comes down in the bread and wine of Holy Communion. (God comes down in bread and wine to fill your hearts with love and peace — and give you the strength to share that love and peace with others.) God comes down when people feel sorrow and regret for their mistakes. God comes down when we learn to forgive and when enemies are reconciled to each other. God comes down when we feel anger at injustice in the world and work for peace and justice. God comes down when warring nations learn to live together in peace. God comes down when we learn to love our neighbor who is different from us. God comes down bringing the beloved community of peace and harmony.

Martin Luther King Jr. had a dream, a vision of the beloved community that God brings down to our world. That dream still inspires us today. I get inspired every time I hear his "I Have a Dream" speech, because I know that Dr. King was giving voice to the same hopes and dreams that the prophet John was describing. God is calling us to live our lives by that dream, the vision of heaven coming down to earth to make all things new. God is calling us today to follow the lamb and rely on lamb power to change our world.

The fires in California have been devastating. There has been a tragic loss of life. Paradise, California, may have burned down, but it isn't gone. It can be rebuilt, and it will be rebuilt. In the aftermath of a fire, in the midst of the ashes, new life springs forth. Haven't you seen it in the ditches along the highway when we burn the grass and the weeds? The next spring, new life comes forth. God comes down and out of the ashes makes everything new. That is what God has promised. "Behold, I am making all things new." God can do that in Paradise, California. God can do that in your heart and in mine.

Suggested Prayer of the Day — ELW Sixth Sunday of Easter C
Suggested Opening Hymn — "The Church's One Foundation"
Suggested Hymn of the Day — "Alleluia! Jesus is Risen"
Suggested Closing Hymn — "Soon and Very Soon"

#12 – Back to the Future: Revelation 21:9-12, 15-16, 21-27; 22:1-7

Today is Christ the King Sunday. It is a Sunday that orients us to the future when Christ comes again to establish a reign of justice and peace. Instead of focusing on the past, this Sunday points us to the future.

Many people today have an intense interest in the past. How many of you have had your DNA tested? There is a curiosity to know where we come from and what our DNA might tell us about who we are. Of course, we aren't just the product of our DNA. We are also a product of our environment and how our parents raised us. We know that the past influences us, but on this Christ the King Sunday we are being taught to look at ourselves through a different lens, not through the past, but through the future. It isn't just the past that influences us. The future influences us as well. And as people of faith, we believe that Christ will come again to establish a reign of justice and peace. That belief shapes us today, our words, our actions, our values and ethics.

I learned an interesting word — prolepsis. Prolepsis is "the assumption of a future act as if presently existing." So, let me give you a few examples of what I mean by prolepsis. Prolepsis is knowing that your baby is going to arrive in just a few months. That knowledge of the future influences your present. Prolepsis is also knowing that you aren't going to live forever. Someday you will die and with that knowledge, you write your will and get your affairs in order. Maybe you downsize and start to get rid of things. That too is what prolepsis is — the future impacting and shaping our present.

I have one last example of prolepsis. Have you ever seen the movie *Back to the Future*? Who doesn't love Michael J. Fox and that cool souped-up DeLorean? And the whole premise of the movie is that someone from the future goes back thirty years into the past and then has to find a way back to the future. He knows what is going to happen in the future and is able to reassure others with that knowledge, and to encourage them not to give up hope. You see, that's what prolepsis is - knowing the future and letting that shape how we live our lives in the present.

Prolepsis is how the church year ends with Christ the King Sunday. It also is how the Bible ends with the book of Revelation. The prophet John gives us a vision of the future. He was writing at a time of great stress to give a word of hope and encouragement to Christians living then. Don't give up. Don't despair. Don't become jaded and cynical and think that things will never change, never get better. Don't let your past determine your present. Instead let the future shape your present. No matter how bad things get, Christ is coming again to establish a reign of justice and righteousness and peace.

In the last two chapters of Revelation, John gives us a foretaste of what is coming. What will the future reign of Christ look like? He wants that vision to change the way we view our world and our place in it.

John takes us on a tour of the New Jerusalem. The first thing we notice on this tour are the pearly gates. We have a lot of fun with those pearly gates jokes. But the jokes often get it wrong. In the jokes, the gates are closed and we have to pass some test in order to get in. But the prophet John shows us something else. God's coming kingdom has twelve gates. Now, gates were important in ancient times for keeping bad things out and protecting the people of the city. The gates of the New Jerusalem are made of pearls and they are never shut. The pearly gates aren't there to keep people out, but to let people in. As we enter in through the gates, we find we are not alone. People from every nation enter. This is not a place for the privileged few, like in ancient Roman society. Rich and poor alike enter to bring God their glory. They are not defeated subjects forced to pay taxes and tribute, but grateful servants come to worship God.

The second thing we notice on our tour is that God's kingdom is a city. The Bible begins in a garden, with Adam and Eve. It ends with a city. That tells us that our relationship with God, though personal, is never private. We are part of a community from every tribe and people, from every language and nation. And there is something else interesting about this city. This city has some unusual dimensions. John describes it shaped like a cube, roughly 1,500 miles wide and deep and high. Again, this is hard to imagine, but there is a deeper meaning here. John was steeped in the Old Testament where the Holy of Holies in the Jerusalem temple was a perfect cube. It was the place where God's glory lived and where only the high priest could enter once a year. So, in describing heaven as a perfect cube, John is implying that God lives here. God's glory fills it.

As we continue to tour the city, we walk about without a care or worry. If you've ever worried how safe it is to walk outside at night, this is one city you will never have to fear. "Nothing unclean will enter it, nor anyone who practices abomination or falsehood, but only those who are written in the lamb's book of life" (Revelations 21:27). There is no night, no darkness for bad things to hide in. There is no need for the moon or sun. The light of God's glory fills the city. What John wants to tell us is that heaven will be a place of safety.

As we tour the city, we notice gold and precious gems everywhere. The street we are walking on "is pure gold, transparent as glass." How can gold be transparent? Here is another example where John doesn't mean what he says - he means what he means. This city is a place of abundance instead of the scarcity of the Roman Empire. Rome provided plenty of benefits for the rich, while the poor struggled for life's essentials. In heaven's economy, gold is so plentiful they pave the streets with it. Everyone shares in the abundance.

Going further in the city, we see a garden, and in the midst of the garden flows the river of life. In ancient times, water was an essential part of a city's security and defense. You can't endure a long siege without water. Cities would build long tunnel systems just to be able to access water without going outside the walls. But in the New Jerusalem, a river flows through the city. Water is abundant and available to all. It is the water of life, water freely available to all. Twice in the book of Revelation, we are told to drink the water of life as a gift. We don't need money to buy it. God gives it freely to all. This water quenches the thirst in our bodies and quenches the thirst of our souls.

On either side of the river we see the tree of life. John tells us something interesting about this tree. It bears fruit each month. Again, it is an image of abundance. There is a harvest to be had all year round and no time when there is scarcity. Fall is harvest time. We reap the fruits of our gardens and fields. In ancient times, people had to preserve food to eat the rest of the year. People who lived through the Great Depression knew scarcity. They canned fruit and produce from the garden just to make sure there would be plenty throughout the year. That's what you did to survive. But John wants us to know that in this place, the tree of life produces fruit each month, food plentiful throughout the year. And the leaves of this tree have medicinal properties. They are for the healing of the nations. We are invited to sit in the shade of this tree and place its leaves in every wound we have, physical, emotional and spiritual. I think that all of us bear wounds and scars of one kind or another. Where are we to find healing from life's hurts and sorrows? The leaves have the power to heal our deepest brokenness. John reminded us that the tree of life is there for our healing. God's kingdom is not built on violence and coercion, but on healing and restoration.

Now we come to the highlight of our tour. There in the center of the city is the throne of God. You don't need an appointment to see God. Everyone has access to God all the time for God's glory fills the city. I love the verse that says, "the throne of God and of the lamb will be in it, and his servants will worship him; they will see his face, and his name will be on their foreheads" (Revelations 22:3-4). In the Old Testament, to see God's face was to die. But not in the New Jerusalem. As we approach the throne, God's glory gets brighter and brighter. We might start to get a bit scared or nervous. What will it be like to see the almighty and holy God? But there is something compelling about the throne. The light draws us into God's presence. God's glory is reassuring as we realize that God's holiness blazes with love. As we draw closer, we see the face of Jesus, the lamb of God. His eyes look into our eyes. They know everything about us, all the sin and brokenness of our past. His eyes are filled with compassion. He's not interested in punishing us. He is interested in healing our wounds. There at the throne we all look God full in the face, and instead of dying from terror, we find healing. In the gaze from God's eyes we leave behind our guilt and shame, and instead experience God's freedom, joy, and peace.

Our brief tour of the New Jerusalem is ended. We get just a small taste. There is so much more to see and experience. It is a most beautiful place. Would you like to come again? Would you like to live in this city? I would. That is exactly what John wants to happen in us. John called on Christians to come out of Babylon, to come out of Rome and resist its violent and unjust empire. But John needed a place to call people to. The New Jerusalem is a vision of the future that God will provide. That vision is still calling us today, calling us from the future to make our world a better place, to make our world more like the place where Christ reigns.

When Jesus taught his disciples to pray, he told them to pray that God's will "be done, on earth as it is in heaven." If we want to know what kind of world God wants us to try to make, we need only look at this vision of the New Jerusalem to learn the values at the heart of God. There are no categories of rich or poor in God's kingdom. One race is not better than another. Men and women are treated the same. There is plenty for everyone. No one goes hungry. All have what they need. We are all beloved and all stand on the same ground at the foot of the cross. We are all sinners who have been given extravagant grace.

There is a wonderful hymn in our hymnal called, "I Want to Walk as a Child of the Light." It was written by Kathleen Thomerson. Because it is still under copyright law, you will have to look up the lyrics online or in a hymnal. She borrows language from Revelation 22 and writes a prayer expressing the deep yearning of our hearts to look in the face of God and find forgiveness and love.

The book of Revelation ends with Jesus saying that he is coming again soon. This is the future that is calling to us now, informing our lives and our values, shaping how we see the world and each other. This is a vision of hope for our world. The response of those first Christians was to say a prayer, **"Amen. Come Lord Jesus!"** We pray that Jesus will come again soon with his truth and justice and love to redeem our world.

Suggested Prayer of the Day — ELW Christ the King B

Suggested Opening Hymn — "All Hail the Power of Jesus' Name"

Suggested Hymn of the Day — "I Want to Walk as a Child of the Light"

Suggested Closing Hymn — "Shall We Gather at the River?"

Possible Worship Elements For A Revelation Preaching Series

CONFESSION AND FORGIVENESS

Grace to you and peace from him who is and who was and who is to come, and from the seven spirits who are before his throne, and from Jesus Christ, the faithful witness, the firstborn of the dead, and the ruler of the kings of the earth (1:4-5).

Amen.

Come out of her, my people, so that you do not take part in her sins (18:4). Listen! I am standing at the door, knocking; if you hear my voice and open the door, I will come in to you and eat with you, and you with me (3:20).

(Silence for reflection)

Salvation and glory and power to our God, for his judgments are true and just (19:1). We confess, O Lord, that our love for you has grown lukewarm (3:16). We have grown complacent in accepting injustice, too afraid to speak out. We have been seduced by the love of things instead of love for you, the creator of all things. In our pursuit of wealth, we have despoiled your beautiful creation. Turn us again from our sins, O Lord, to follow you alone, that we may experience your blessing.

To him who loves us and freed us from our sins by his blood and made us to be a kingdom, priests serving his God and Father, to him be glory and dominion forever and ever (1:5-6).

Amen.

The one who is seated on the throne says, "See, I am making all things new. These words are trustworthy and true. I am the Alpha and the Omega, the beginning and the end. To the thirsty I will give water as a gift from the spring of the water of life. I will be their God and they will be my children" (21:5-7).

Amen.

REVELATION LITURGY

There in heaven stood a throne with one seated on the throne. Around the throne are 24 thrones with 24 elders, dressed in white robes, with golden crowns on their heads (4:2-4). The 24 elders fall before the one who is seated on the throne and worship the one who lives forever and ever; they cast their crowns before the throne singing, (4:10)

" Holy, holy, holy, Lord God Almighty!

Then I saw between the throne and among the elders a lamb standing as if it had been slaughtered. The 24 elders fell before the lamb. Joining them was the voice of many angels surrounding the throne numbering myriads of myriads and thousands of thousands. And every creature in heaven and on earth and under the earth and in the sea, and all that is in them, together were singing: (5:6, 8, 11, 13), "

(Sing the hymn, "Worthy is Christ, the Lamb Who Was Slain.")

PRAYERS OF INTERCESSION

An angel with a golden censer came and stood at the altar; he was given a great quantity of incense to offer with the prayers of all the saints on the golden altar that is before the throne. And the smoke of the incense, with the prayers of the saints, rose before God from the hand of the angel. (8:3-4) Let us pray for the church, for the needs of the poor, and for the whole creation.

Offering Hymn 433, "Blessing, Honor, and Glory"

Offering Prayer
You are worthy, our Lord and God, to receive glory and honor and power, for you created all things (4:11). You gather us at the river of life to quench our thirst. You feed us from the tree of life for our healing (22:1-2). Use the gifts we offer now that we might join you in bringing your healing to all the nations, through Jesus Christ, our Lord. Amen.

Invitation To Communion

Blessed are those who are invited to the marriage supper of the lamb. These are true words of God (19:9).

Eucharistic Prayer

It is indeed right to give you our thanks and praise, O God, for the glorious resurrection of our Savior Jesus Christ. He is the lamb who was slaughtered (5:6) and freed us from our sins by his blood, who in dying has destroyed the powers of death, and in rising has brought us to eternal life. And so, with earth and sea and all their creatures, and with angels and archangels, cherubim and seraphim, we praise your name and join their unending hymn: (5:11-14)

Holy, holy, holy, the Lord God the Almighty, who was and is and is to come (4:8). Heaven and earth are full of your glory. Hosanna in the highest.

God of our weary years, God of our silent tears, you have brought us this far along the way.[106]

In times of bitterness you did not abandon us but guided us into the path of love and light.

In every age you sent prophets to make known your loving will for all humanity. The cry of the poor has become your own cry; our hunger and thirst for justice is your own desire. In the fullness of time, you sent your chosen servant to preach good news to the afflicted, to break bread with the outcast and despised, and to ransom those in bondage to prejudice and sin.

In the night in which he was betrayed, our Lord Jesus took bread, and gave thanks; broke it, and gave it to his disciples, saying: Take and eat; this is my body, given for you. Do this for the remembrance of me. Again, after supper, he took the cup, gave thanks, and gave it for all to drink, saying: This cup is the new covenant in my blood, shed for you and all people for the forgiveness of sin. Do this for the remembrance of me.

For as often as we eat of this bread and drink from this cup,

106 The following Eucharistic Prayer is from *Evangelical Lutheran Worship*. Minneapolis: Augsburg Fortress, 2019. Used by permission

we proclaim the Lord's death until he comes.

Christ has died. Christ is risen. Christ will come again.

Remembering, therefore, his death and resurrection, we await the day when Jesus shall return to free all the earth from the bonds of slavery and death. Come, Lord Jesus! And let the church say, Amen…

Amen.

Send your Holy Spirit, our advocate, to fill the hearts of all who share this bread and cup with courage and wisdom to pursue love and justice in all the world. Come, Spirit of freedom! And let the church say, Amen…

Amen.

Join our prayers and praise with your prophets and martyrs of every age, that, rejoicing in the hope of the resurrection, we might live in the freedom and hope of your son. Through him, with him, in him, in the unity of the Holy Spirit, all glory and honor is yours, almighty Father, now and forever.

Amen.

Post Communion Hymn 439, "Soon and Very Soon"

Benediction

To everyone who conquers, I will give permission to eat from the tree of life that is in the paradise of God.

Let anyone who has an ear listen to what the Spirit is saying to the churches.

The Spirit and the bride say, "Come."

And let everyone who hears say, "Come."

And let everyone who is thirsty come.

Let anyone who wishes take the water of life as a gift.

The one who testifies to these things says, "Surely I am coming soon."

Amen. Come, Lord Jesus!

The grace of the Lord Jesus be with all the saints. Amen.

Oral Performance Of The Book Of Revelation

"Blessed Is The One Who Reads Aloud The Words Of The Prophecy"

As we have seen in Chapter 2, several tools are available to preachers to discover meaning in the book of Revelation. In this chapter, we will explore further a narrative approach to the book. David Barr has argued that the oral and aural experience of the apocalypse is "an essential element of its hermeneutic."[107] Preachers, who are serious about engaging the message of Revelation today, will want to give some thought to how we hear Revelation as story. How can congregations be equipped to hear the whole narrative meaningfully so that God's Spirit may speak in new ways through this ancient witness?

Revelation was originally written to be read aloud in the context of worship. Much of the language of Revelation is the language of worship. "The apocalypse is primarily an experience, more particularly an experience of worship. Thus its consistent theme to worship God is self-actualizing: when one hears these words one is doing them."[108] Some scholars even detect in the language of the final chapter a segue into the celebration of the eucharist.[109]

How would an oral or dramatic performance change the hearers' encounter with Revelation, as opposed to an individualistic reading of the story from the pages of the Bible? Does the communal context of worship shape that encounter in fundamental ways? Barr believes that "the oral performance of the apocalypse served to make Jesus present…. The prophet stands

107 David L. Barr, "The Apocalypse of John as Oral Enactment,"
Interpretation 40 (1986), 243.
108 Barr, *Tales of the End: A Narrative Commentary on the Book of Revelation*, 171.
109 Boring, *Revelation*, 6.

in the place of Jesus and makes him present to the community; the public reader stands in the place of the prophet and makes him (and Jesus) present."Barr argues that the central theme of the apocalypse was the proper worship of God, and that it portrayed a struggle between the worship of God and the worship of Satan. The oral enactment of Revelation did more than just describe to worshipers the coming kingdom of God; it brings them the kingdom:

> As a story the apocalypse has the power to take us in, to transport us into a new world. As an enacted story the apocalypse has the power to bring into existence that reality which it portrays, to transform the finite province of meaning into the paramount reality of those who worship. It becomes a charter story that establishes a new world in which God triumphs over evil through the death of Jesus and the suffering of his followers. Because the kingdom of God is his true worship, the very enactment of the Apocalypse establishes that kingdom in this world.[110]

Hearing the story is a profound experience with the power to transform members of the community.

Stanley Saunders made a similar argument that an oral presentation of the apocalypse is meant to transform its hearers. He maintains that this was an important tool in shaping alternative imaginations and practices that could resist the dominant narrative of the Roman Empire:

> In short, the apocalypse is not merely an argument, but an oral performance that generates an array of experiences and reactions, thereby to transform the social space inhabited by both performer and audience…. Were we more accustomed to hearing the apocalypse performed as a whole in our modern assemblies, as it likely was in the eucharistic assemblies of congregations in Asia Minor during the last half of the first century,

110 Ibid, 256.

we would have a more immediate and powerful sense of the ways this work alters imagination, calls forth new social bodies and practices, and evokes surprising new visions of the world."[111]

It should not be surprising that an oral performance today would have a similar impact on congregations.

Essentials for Hearing the Story of Revelation

Several things make it difficult for modern people to hear Revelation as story. Since the book is part of the Bible, people tend to bring to this story a different set of expectations than if they had purchased a book of fiction at Barnes & Noble. Its status as inspired scripture predisposes some to view Revelation as propositional speech or future prediction. These hermeneutical presuppositions treat the interpretation of Revelation "as story" with suspicion. The fact that Revelation is divided into chapters and verses (that were not part of the original) allows the story to be more easily dissected into bits and pieces for study, rather than experienced as a narrative whole. Because some of Revelation's images, such as the millennium or the mark of the beast, are encrusted with layers of interpretation in the popular culture, people have more difficulty hearing the story afresh. Finally, Revelation uses an obscure set of images and symbols modern people do not identify with as easily. All these factors make it more difficult to hear Revelation as narrative. An oral reading in one sitting could go a long way towards overcoming these impediments.

In his book, *Tales of the End: A Narrative Commentary on the Book of Revelation*, author David Barr tries to define "what is necessary for a modern American reader to enable her or him to hear the story of the apocalypse."[112] What essentials would help a worshipping community today experience the story and encounter the Christ to whom the story points? Barr mentions the following:

111 Saunders, "Revelation and Resistance: Narrative and Worship in John's Apocalypse." 124-5.
112 Barr, *Tales of the End: A Narrative Commentary on the Book of Revelation*, 1.

Minimal preliminaries include having some sense of what the story is about (content), some clues as to how this content is being communicated (form), a general notion of how this material is arranged (structure and plot), an orientation to the characters in the story — including its audience (characterization), some sense of the meaning of the strange creatures and mystical numbers we encounter (symbolization), and a placing of the story in time and geography (setting).[113]

These minimal preliminaries will be summarized in the following pages. The author is deeply indebted to Dr. Barr. We will now look briefly at each of these elements.

The Content of the Story

The first clue as to the content of Revelation's story is given in the first verse: "the revelation of Jesus Christ." The basic story underlying Revelation is the story of Jesus. The apocalypse is the revelation "of" Jesus Christ, because he performs the central role in the story:

> The recognition that the narrative of Revelation is about Jesus (not about the future or about the United States and Russia or about puzzles to solve) is for me the crucial insight for understanding this work.... To understand the apocalypse we must always keep clearly in mind the struggle of Jesus with the evil powers of this world, their unremitting destruction of him, and his ultimate vindication — a vindication expressed by early believers as his resurrection from the dead and/or being raised to share the throne of God. The apocalypse is in its most basic sense a retelling of this story of Jesus in a new way and with new images.[114]

While the content of the story of Revelation is the story of

113 Ibid, 1-2.
114 Ibid, 3.

Jesus, it must be said that there are few connections between Revelation's Jesus and the historical Jesus of the gospels. In Revelation, Jesus' death and resurrection are the main connection to the historical Jesus, a feature shared with many of the epistles. In 1 Corinthians 15:3-4, the apostle Paul listed those elements of the Christ story he considers of first importance, "that Christ died for our sins in accordance with the scriptures, and that he was buried, and that he was raised on the third day." Revelation shares with this passage these brief, yet essential, connections to the historical Jesus.

The Genre of Revelation

The first word of John's Revelation illuminated what type of literature it was. Apocalypse was a well-known literary genre in the ancient world. A familiarity with other apocalypses and their common features helps us to understand the strange world of Revelation.

Apocalypses often begin with a dream or a vision. Next, a transportation to heaven occurs where the seer is taught the true meaning of what is seen. This is often marked by strange and incomprehensible figures such as bizarre animals, colors and numbers. All these signal the reading an apocalypse, a highly symbolic form of writing. Some symbols were well-known; others John explained himself. The important thing to remember is that the world of Revelation was pregnant and bursting with significance. Things meant things:

> We must never stop at the surface meaning of the text. What we see and hear are signs whose significance lies on some other level. The simple notion that a text means what it says is always inadequate, but with Revelation is always wrong. Revelation does not mean what it says, it means what it means. It is a book of signs.[115]

Keeping in mind that the Revelation to John fits into this well-known genre known as apocalypse will give us clues as to how

115 Ibid, 4.

to hear and properly interpret its story.

Symbols in Revelation

Revelation is a multimedia world filled with strange sights and sounds. Often what is seen interprets what is heard, as is the case with the lion/lamb found in chapter 5. Over the centuries, visual artists have tried to depict its strange symbols. However, many of Revelation's symbols are better heard than seen. For example, the beast with seven heads and ten horns is difficult to see. How does one fit them all in? It is easier to hear what is meant: the seven heads represent complete authority, and ten horns represent total power. Our basic interpretive principle is that Revelation does not mean what it says, but means what it means. So how is one to know what Revelation's symbols mean?

John himself gave us the meaning to several of the symbols he uses. In 1:20, John identified the seven stars as the angels of the seven churches, and the seven lampstands are the seven churches themselves. Several more instances occur where John explained the symbols he used.

One place to look for insight is other literature of the period, particularly other apocalypses and prophetic writings. John is well-versed in the literature of his day and makes extensive allusions to these writings in his book. John's audience would have been familiar with this symbolic network.

Three standard categories of symbols were widely used in apocalypses, including numbers, animals, and colors, that would have had standardized and understood meanings. Many commentaries have valuable charts and tables exploring these symbols. "Grasping the significance of John's elemental symbolism will prevent the most naïve kind of misreading and will prepare us to encounter the more dynamic symbolism of the narrative."[116] A brief exploration of these stock numbers, animals and colors would be helpful for modern congregations to understand layers of meaning intended by the author.

Symbols, by definition, should not be interpreted literally. The images in Revelation are best grasped with the imagination than

116 Ibid, 9.

with the mind. "A symbol does not so much mean something as it does imply, so deciphering symbols is less a rational act than an imaginative act. It is thus of the utmost importance that we read the apocalypse with our imaginations engaged."[117] Like the facets of a diamond, symbols open up multiple windows of meaning. Symbols are polyvalent; they speak on multiple levels at the same time, like the notes of a musical chord. The woman clothed with the sun in chapter 12 could be Eve or she could be Mary. She could be Israel or the church. Symbols allow us to express what we could not express in ordinary words. For instance, the symbol of a burning flag can open up many layers of meaning, interpreted in different ways by different people. "Symbols do not simply carry information; they reach out and take hold of us, demand our attention. John's book has that power once we prepare ourselves to receive its symbolic speech."[118] Symbols reach us at a different level than ordinary speech, and are thus capable of communicating with great power.

Structure and Plot

The apocalypse is a complex story and no scholarly consensus exists on how to organize its content. How one arranges the material depends on what one is searching for in the first place. Barr suggests that when looking for the storyline in Revelation, a reasonably clear pattern emerges. He sees a strong correlation between the beginning (1:1-17) and the end (22:6-21), a common feature in good stories. Between these bookends, he discerns three distinct and interrelated movements. The first (chapters 1-3) was a theophany, a revelation of a divine figure, who dictated to John seven messages to the angels of seven churches. In the second movement (chapters 4-11), John was taken up to heaven where he saw a vision of the throne of God. A lamb that was slain opened a divine scroll and revealed its contents. The third movement (chapters 12-22) was the story of a cosmic war. A dragon pursued a woman, but was eventually defeated by a warrior, resulting in the establishment of a new cosmic order. While Barr claims

117 Ibid
118 Ibid, 10.

that no real narrative connection exists between these three movements, he asserts that we do not have three different stories. "They represent alternative tellings of the story of Jesus with a common theme and overlapping characters…. Rather than one unfolding event, Revelation presents three interrelated tellings of the story of Jesus."[119] By appearing together, the three gain meaning they would not have as single stories.

Characters

The action in Revelation takes place on two different planes, namely in heaven and on earth, where one meets the expected sort of characters. In heaven, one encounters God, Jesus, the Spirit, angels and the dead. On earth, one meets John, the churches, Antipas, Jezebel, kings, merchants, and ordinary people. In John's story, one also meets the unexpected: a lamb standing as if slain, a great dragon, a woman clothed with the sun, grotesque beasts, a heavenly warrior, a representative whore and a bride. Three movements of the narrative plot contain three separate sets of characters. A main character appears in each movement: the exalted son of man, the lamb, and the rider on a white horse. Some overlap happens with characters from one movement appearing in another. For example, the beast of the third movement appears briefly in the second, as does the army of 144,000. The lamb of the second movement appears in the third. This overlapping of characters in the three movements can offer new levels of meaning. The image of a lamb at the head of an army may give insight into the kind of war that is waged. New insights may be gained by tracking how the characters function at each point in the story.

Time and Place

The action in Revelation seems to happen in one day. John received his vision on "the Lord's day" (Revelation 1:10). The use of time throughout Revelation, however, is quite fluid and highly symbolic. It is helpful for the reader to differentiate between story time and historical time. As Barr admonished, "We

119 Ibid, 15.

must take seriously the fact that we are reading a narrative work and not naïvely assume that the times and places we read of in the story are the actual times and places of the audience of the work."[120] Having said this, the seven cities mentioned are real historical cities that were located in the Roman province of Asia. John demonstrated an intimate knowledge of local conditions in the area.

Archaeological and literary sources reveal a great deal of information about this area. Six out of the seven cities were capitals of their respective regions. The first and second centuries were prosperous times in that region of Asia. This prosperity, however, was not evenly shared beyond an elite minority tied to Rome. The region was prone to rebellion by subjects tired of high taxes and Roman domination. Many of these cities had shrines to promote the Roman imperial cult. Loyalty and patriotism to the state were expressed by offering worship to Caesar. Revelation, therefore, urged Christians to resist the blasphemous claims of Roman imperial authority.

Scholars disagree as to the situation of Christians reflected in Revelation. One position is that some deliberate persecution of Christians existed. Others argue that there was little if any persecution, and that John was writing to urge faithfulness among those seduced by the Roman Empire and its values.

The dating of the book is debated, although most scholars place it at the end of the first century, around 96 AD. An earlier date in the late sixties is sometimes argued because of the probable references to Emperor Nero (15-68 AD). Rather than assuming that John received his vision in one day, Revelation may reflect the visions of a decades-long ministry that achieved their final form near the end of the first century.

Making an Interpretation

There are as many interpretations as there are interpreters. Discuss a movie with someone and one will find that each has a different interpretation of the same story. That is because everyone interprets stories differently depending on the questions and

120 Ibid, 20.

presuppositions they bring. Stories are capable of more than one interpretation, but not all interpretations are equally valid. As Barr wrote, "All interpretations that are grounded in what a text actually says are to some degree valid…. While a given text might not determine our reading, it does constrain it."[121] For example, some see in John's journey into heaven in chapter 4 a reference to the rapture of the church. The word, "rapture," is not used in Revelation. In fact, the concept of a rapture, a supernatural rescue of God's people from a time of tribulation, is foreign to the basic storyline of revelation. This interpretation violates the ordinary reading of the text and will be recognized as wrong.

The story of Revelation is meant to be an experience that transforms rather than a source of information or doctrine. The book was meant to be experienced aurally in the context of worship rather than studied on a page. It is the author's hope that congregations today will find ways to hear this story and be moved to faithfully worship God and the lamb.

A Dramatic Reading Proposal

How does one actually go about presenting the story of Revelation? Would modern people attend an event where the book is read aloud? Reading Revelation from beginning to end could take two hours. Can a reading of the whole story sustain the attention of modern people? Are there special things congregations today can do to facilitate the encounter with the text?

The following is a dramatic reading of an edited version of the book of Revelation. For the sake of brevity, I have chosen to eliminate portions of the book that were less critical to its overall message and impact. I have divided the text into four speaking parts: the narrator John, Jesus, a generic voice, and the congregation. Instead of the entire book being read by one person, the speaking parts are divided in this proposal. Involving the congregation in this way can help to keep it engaged and attentive. Interspersed throughout are well-known and beloved

121 Ibid, 22-3.

hymns whose words have been inspired by Revelation. This proposal keeps the congregation involved through active participation. The order also gives the feel of a worship service, with hymns, readings, and sermon.

One of the logistical difficulties with this proposal is how to get the speaking parts delivered to the congregation at the appropriate time. There are two options: either print out the whole dramatic reading in a booklet for the congregation to follow, or project those words the congregation is being asked to speak. The second option seems preferable. Reading something on a page diminishes the impact of the experience. This is analogous to watching a foreign language film and reading the subtitles, or attending a play and instead of watching the actors, following the script. One is not as involved in the experience. Copyright issues are also involved in reproducing extended passages from any version of the Bible.

Interrupting the story with hymns gives an opportunity for the hymn texts to offer a commentary. Revelation has inspired more music than almost any other book of the Bible. Hymns help to interpret the narrative by including the history of interpretation (see chapter 2 — the world around the text) as companion to the story. Familiar hymns also bring a note of comfort and legitimacy to those hearers, who may regard Revelation with some skepticism or fear:

> One of the greatest barriers that people face when opening Revelation is the fear of being confused or misled by its images. People may overcome some of this uneasiness when they realize that Revelation's most abiding contribution has not been to stir people into a frenzy over the date of Christ's return, but to give communities of faith some of the language that they have used for generations when giving praise to God and the Lamb.... Moreover, the hymns lift up passages that stress hope, joy, and faithfulness. Readers cannot

ignore Revelation's many warnings about divine judgment, but the worship scenes help readers interpret the warnings in light of the promises, and to understand that God's purposes are directed toward the joy of salvation.[122]

Singing these well-known and beloved hymns can be a reassuring presence in a narrative filled with confusing and foreboding images. "Readers will encounter many threatening images in Revelation, but those who keep the musical scenes in mind will not lose sight of the book's goal."[123]

Including hymns in a reading of Revelation mirrors the story itself, which interjects all kinds of hymn-like materials into the action (Revelation 4:8-11, 5:9-13, 7:10-11, 11:15-18, 12:10-12, 15:3-4, 19:1-8). The reenactment of Revelation is meant to be a worship experience. The worship passages in Revelation often come at the end of a narrative pattern of seven, resembling the weekly pattern of the community gathering for worship every seventh day. This narrative device itself gives witness to the importance of weekly worship to reorient the community around God's truth and renew the church's commitment to faithful witness.

If congregations have projection capability, they may want to add a further dimension to the experience. Revelation has inspired great visual artists throughout the ages who have interpreted its story. By projecting selected images at appropriate times in the reading, the worship experience can be enhanced. Planners will need to be sensitive to the use of art. Because of the highly symbolic nature of Revelation, many of its images are better grasped by the imagination than by the eyes. A literal depiction of a beast with seven heads and ten horns may cause one to laugh at its absurdity. Images that open up the imagination, rather than close it off, are preferable.

Many Revelation images are readily available on the internet. Websites such as www.biblical-art.com allow searches for images based on the biblical text. Felix Just has a website with a page of links to Revelation art organized by collections or by biblical

---

122 Koester, *Revelation and the End of All Things*, 38.
123 Ibid, 40.

text.[124] Copyright laws will need to be followed in the use of these images. One particularly helpful resource is the Bamberg Apocalypse, an eleventh-century illuminated manuscript with over fifty images that are in the public domain.

124 Felix Just, "Art, Images, Music and Materials Related to the Book of Revelation," Catholic-Resources.org http://catholic-resources.org/Art/Revelation-Art.htm (accessed January 13, 2008).

A Dramatic Reading Of The Book Of Revelation

(In this dramatic narrative there are four readers — the narrator, an unseen generic voice, Jesus, and the congregation. The setting of Revelation moves between earth and heaven. This movement can be reflected in the place the narrator reads from. Moving the narrator from the congregation level to the level of the chancel or altar can reflect this shift in location. The narrative begins with the narrator and Jesus in the midst of the congregation. Seven lampstands or candlestands should be set among the congregation with the names of the seven churches on them. Three of the seven letters will be read at the appropriate candlestand. The reading is interspersed with the singing of hymns. An abbreviated recording of the "Hallelujah Chorus" may be played in two appropriate places.)

Hymn: "All Hail the Power of Jesus' Name" (in the public domain)

Act 1 — The Letter Scroll

Narrator: The revelation of Jesus Christ, which God gave him to show his servants what must soon take place; he made it known by sending his angel to his servant John, who testified to the word of God and to the testimony of Jesus Christ, even to all that he saw.

All: Blessed is the one who reads aloud the words of the prophecy and blessed are those who hear and who keep what is written in it; for the time is near.

Narrator: John to the seven churches that are in Asia: Grace to you and peace from him who is and who was and who is to come, and from the seven spirits who are before his throne, and from Jesus Christ, the faithful witness, the firstborn of the dead, and the ruler of the kings of the earth. To him who loves us,

All: and freed us from our sins by his blood, and made us to be a kingdom, priests serving his God and Father, to him be glory and dominion forever and ever. Amen.

Narrator: Look! He is coming with the clouds; every eye will see him, even those who pierced him; and on his account all the tribes of the earth will wail. So it is to be. Amen.

Voice: "I am the Alpha and the Omega,"

Narrator: Says the Lord God, who is and who was and who is to come, the almighty.

Narrator: I, John, your brother who share with you in Jesus the persecution and the kingdom and the patient endurance, was on the island called Patmos because of the word of God and the testimony of Jesus. I was in the spirit on the Lord's day, and I heard behind me a loud voice like a trumpet saying,

Voice: "Write in a book what you see and send it to the seven churches, to Ephesus, to Smyrna, to Pergamum, to Thyatira, to Sardis, to Philadelphia, and to Laodicea."

Narrator: Then I turned to see whose voice it was that spoke to me, and on turning I saw seven golden lampstands, and in the midst of the lampstands I saw one like the Son of Man, clothed with a long robe and with a golden sash across his chest. His head and his hair were white as white wool, white as snow; his eyes were like a flame of fire, his feet were like burnished bronze, refined as in a furnace, and his voice was like the sound of many waters. In his right hand he held seven stars, and from his mouth came a sharp, two-edged sword, and his face was like the sun shining with full force. When I saw him, I fell at his feet as though dead. But he placed his right hand on me, saying,

Jesus: "Do not be afraid; I am the first and the last, and the living one. I was dead, and see, I am alive forever and ever; and I have the keys of death and of Hades. Now write what you have seen, what is, and what is to take place after this. As for the mystery of the seven stars that you saw in my right hand, and the seven golden lampstands: the seven stars are the angels of the seven churches, and the seven lampstands are the seven churches.

Voice: "To the angel of the church in Ephesus write: These are the words of him who holds the seven stars in his right hand, who walks among the seven golden lampstands:

Jesus: *(at the first candlestand)* "I know your works, your toil and your patient endurance. I know that you cannot tolerate evildoers; you have tested those who claim to be apostles but are not and have found them to be false. I also know that you are enduring patiently and bearing up for the sake of my name, and that you have not grown weary. But I have this against you, that you have abandoned the love you had at first. Remember then from what you have fallen; repent, and do the works you did at first. If not, I will come to you and remove your lampstand from its place, unless you repent. Yet this is to your credit: you hate the works of the Nicolaitans, which I also hate.

All: Let anyone who has an ear listen to what the Spirit is saying to the churches.

Jesus: To everyone who conquers, I will give permission to eat from the tree of life that is in the paradise of God.

Voice: "And to the angel of the church in Smyrna write: These are the words of the first and the last, who was dead and came to life:

Jesus: *(at the second candlestand)* "I know your affliction and your poverty, even though you are rich. I know the slander on the part of those who say that they are Jews and are not but are a synagogue of Satan. Do not fear what you are about to suffer. Beware, the devil is about to throw some of you into prison so that you may be tested, and for ten days you will have affliction. Be faithful until death, and I will give you the crown of life.

All: Let anyone who has an ear listen to what the Spirit is saying to the churches.

Jesus: Whoever conquers will not be harmed by the second death.

Voice: "And to the angel of the church in Laodicea write: The words of the Amen, the faithful and true witness, the origin of God's creation:

Jesus: *(at the seventh candlestand)* "I know your works; you are neither cold nor hot. I wish that you were either cold or hot.

So, because you are lukewarm, and neither cold nor hot, I am about to spit you out of my mouth. For you say, 'I am rich, I have prospered, and I need nothing.' You do not realize that you are wretched, pitiable, poor, blind, and naked. Therefore I counsel you to buy from me gold refined by fire so that you may be rich; and white robes to clothe you and to keep the shame of your nakedness from being seen; and salve to anoint your eyes so that you may see. I reprove and discipline those whom I love. Be earnest, therefore, and repent. Listen! I am standing at the door, knocking; if you hear my voice and open the door, I will come into you and eat with you, and you with me. To the one who conquers I will give a place with me on my throne, just as I myself conquered and sat down with my Father on his throne.

All: Let anyone who has an ear listen to what the Spirit is saying to the churches."

Hymn: "Holy, Holy, Holy" (still under copyright – look up lyrics)

(The narrator moves up to the chancel/altar level)

Act 2 — The Worship Scroll

Narrator: After this I looked, and there in heaven a door stood open! And the first voice, which I had heard speaking to me like a trumpet, said,

Voice: "Come up here, and I will show you what must take place after this."

Narrator: At once I was in the spirit, and there in heaven stood a throne, with one seated on the throne! And the one seated there looks like jasper and carnelian, and around the throne is a rainbow that looks like an emerald. Around the throne are 24 thrones, and seated on the thrones are 24 elders, dressed in white robes, with golden crowns on their heads. Coming from the throne are flashes of lightning, and rumblings and peals of thunder, and in front of the throne burn seven flaming torches, which are the seven spirits of God; and in front of the throne there is something like a sea of glass, like crystal. Around the throne, and on each side of the throne, are four living creatures, full of eyes in front and behind:

the first living creature like a lion, the second living creature like an ox, the third living creature with a face like a human face, and the fourth living creature like a flying eagle. And the four living creatures, each of them with six wings, are full of eyes all around and inside. Day and night without ceasing they sing,

All: "Holy, holy, holy, the Lord God the Almighty, who was and is and is to come."

Narrator: And whenever the living creatures give glory and honor and thanks to the one who is seated on the throne, who lives forever and ever, the 24 elders fall before the one who is seated on the throne and worship the one who lives forever and ever; they cast their crowns before the throne, singing,

All: "You are worthy, our Lord and God, to receive glory and honor and power, for you created all things, and by your will they existed and were created."

Narrator: Then I saw in the right hand of the one seated on the throne a scroll written on the inside and on the back, sealed with seven seals; and I saw a mighty angel proclaiming with a loud voice,

Voice: "Who is worthy to open the scroll and break its seals?"

Narrator: And no one in heaven or on earth or under the earth was able to open the scroll or to look into it. And I began to weep bitterly because no one was found worthy to open the scroll or to look into it. Then one of the elders said to me,

Voice: "Do not weep. See, the lion of the tribe of Judah, the root of David, has conquered, so that he can open the scroll and its seven seals."

Narrator: Then I saw between the throne and the four living creatures and among the elders a lamb standing as if it had been slaughtered, having seven horns and seven eyes, which are the seven spirits of God sent out into all the earth. He went and took the scroll from the right hand of the one who was seated on the throne. When he had taken the scroll, the four living creatures and the 24 elders fell before the lamb, each holding a harp and golden bowls full of incense, which are the prayers of the saints. They sing a new song:

All: "You are worthy to take the scroll and to open its seals, for you were slaughtered and by your blood you ransomed for God saints from every tribe and language and people and nation; you have made them to be a kingdom and priests serving our God, and they will reign on earth."

Narrator: Then I looked, and I heard the voice of many angels surrounding the throne and the living creatures and the elders; they numbered myriads of myriads and thousands of thousands, singing with full voice,

All: "Worthy is the lamb that was slaughtered to receive power and wealth and wisdom and might and honor and glory and blessing!"

Narrator: Then I heard every creature in heaven and on earth and under the earth and in the sea, and all that is in them, singing,

All: "To the one seated on the throne and to the lamb be blessing and honor and glory and might forever and ever!"

Narrator: And the four living creatures said, "Amen!" And the elders fell down and worshiped.

Hymn: "Blessing And Honor" (Optional: This is the Feast of Victory in the public domain)

(The narrator moves down to the congregation level)

Narrator: Then I saw the lamb open one of the seven seals, and I heard one of the four living creatures call out, as with a voice of thunder,

Voice: "Come!"

Narrator: I looked, and there was a white horse! Its rider had a bow; a crown was given to him, and he came out conquering and to conquer. (*pause*) When he opened the second seal, I heard the second living creature call out,

Voice: "Come!"

Narrator: And out came another horse, bright red; its rider was permitted to take peace from the earth, so that people would slaughter one another; and he was given a great sword. (*pause*) When he opened the third seal, I heard the third living creature call out,

Voice: "Come!"

166

Narrator: I looked, and there was a black horse! Its rider held a pair of scales in his hand, and I heard what seemed to be a voice in the midst of the four living creatures saying,

Voice: "A quart of wheat for a day's pay, and three quarts of barley for a day's pay, but do not damage the olive oil and the wine!"

Narrator: (*pause*) When he opened the fourth seal, I heard the voice of the fourth living creature call out,

Voice: "Come!"

Narrator: I looked and there was a pale green horse! Its rider's name was death, and Hades followed with him; they were given authority over a fourth of the earth, to kill with sword, famine, and pestilence, and by the wild animals of the earth. When he opened the fifth seal, I saw under the altar the souls of those who had been slaughtered for the word of God and for the testimony they had given; they cried out with a loud voice,

All: "Sovereign Lord, holy and true, how long will it be before you judge and avenge our blood on the inhabitants of the earth?"

Narrator: They were each given a white robe and told to rest a little longer, until the number would be complete both of their fellow servants and of their brothers and sisters, who were soon to be killed as they themselves had been killed. When he opened the sixth seal, I looked, and there came a great earthquake; the sun became black as sackcloth, the full moon became like blood, and the stars of the sky fell to the earth as the fig tree drops its winter fruit when shaken by a gale. The sky vanished like a scroll rolling itself up, and every mountain and island was removed from its place. Then the kings of the earth and the magnates and the generals and the rich and the powerful, and everyone, slave and free, hid in the caves and among the rocks of the mountains, calling to the mountains and rocks,

All: "Fall on us and hide us from the face of the one seated on the throne and from the wrath of the lamb; for the great day of their wrath has come, and who is able to stand?"

Hymn: "My Lord, What A Morning" (in the public domain)

(The narrator moves back to the chancel)

Narrator: After this I saw four angels standing at the four corners of the earth, holding back the four winds of the earth so that no wind could blow on earth or sea or against any tree. I saw another angel ascending from the rising of the sun, having the seal of the living God, and he called with a loud voice to the four angels who had been given power to damage earth and sea, saying,

Voice: "Do not damage the earth or the sea or the trees, until we have marked the servants of our God with a seal on their foreheads."

Narrator: And I heard the number of those who were sealed, 144 thousand, sealed out of every tribe of the people of Israel... After this I looked, and there was a great multitude that no one could count, from every nation, from all tribes and peoples and languages, standing before the throne and before the lamb, robed in white, with palm branches in their hands. They cried out in a loud voice, saying,

All: "Salvation belongs to our God who is seated on the throne, and to the lamb!"

Narrator: And all the angels stood around the throne and around the elders and the four living creatures, and they fell on their faces before the throne and worshiped God, singing,

All: "Amen! Blessing and glory and wisdom and thanksgiving and honor and power and might be to our God forever and ever! Amen."

Narrator: Then one of the elders addressed me, saying,

Voice: "Who are these, robed in white, and where have they come from?"

Narrator: I said to him, "Sir, you are the one that knows." Then he said to me,

Voice: "These are they who have come out of the great ordeal; they have washed their robes and made them white in the blood of the lamb. For this reason they are before the throne of God, and worship him day and night within his temple, and the one who is seated on the throne will shelter them. They will hunger no more, and thirst no more; the sun will not strike them, nor any scorching heat; for the lamb at the center of the throne will be their shepherd, and he will guide them to springs of the water of life, and God will wipe away every tear from their eyes."

Narrator: When the lamb opened the seventh seal, there was silence in heaven for about half an hour. (*pause*) And I saw the seven angels who stand before God, and seven trumpets were given to them. Another angel with a golden censer came and stood at the altar; he was given a great quantity of incense to offer with the prayers of all the saints on the golden altar that is before the throne. And the smoke of the incense, with the prayers of the saints, rose before God from the hand of the angel. Then the angel took the censer and filled it with fire from the altar and threw it on the earth; and there were peals of thunder, rumblings, flashes of lightning, and an earthquake.

Hymn: "Ye Servants Of God" (Optional Hymn: Behold A Host – in the public domain)

(The narrator moves to the congregation)

Narrator: Then the voice that I had heard from heaven spoke to me again, saying,

Voice: "Go, take the scroll that is open in the hand of the angel who is standing on the sea and on the land."

Narrator: So I went to the angel and told him to give me the little scroll; and he said to me,

Voice: "Take it and eat; it will be bitter to your stomach, but sweet as honey in your mouth."

Narrator: So I took the little scroll from the hand of the angel and ate it; it was sweet as honey in my mouth, but when I had eaten it, my stomach was made bitter. Then they said to me,

Voice: "You must prophesy again about many peoples and nations and languages and kings."

Narrator: Then I was given a measuring rod like a staff, and I was told,

Voice: "Come and measure the temple of God and the altar and those who worship there, but do not measure the court outside the temple; leave that out, for it is given over to the nations, and they will trample over the holy city for 42 months. And I will grant my two witnesses authority to prophesy for 1,260 days, wearing sackcloth."

Narrator: These are the two olive trees and the two lampstands that stand before the Lord of the earth. And if anyone wants to harm them, fire pours from their mouth and consumes their foes; anyone who wants to harm them must be killed in this manner. They have authority to shut the sky, so that no rain may fall during the days of their prophesying, and they have authority over the waters to turn them into blood, and to strike the earth with every kind of plague, as often as they desire. When they have finished their testimony, the beast that comes up from the bottomless pit will make war on them and conquer them and kill them, and their dead bodies will lie in the street of the great city that is prophetically called Sodom and Egypt, where also their Lord was crucified. For three and a half days members of the peoples and tribes and languages and nations will gaze at their dead bodies and refuse to let them be placed in a tomb; and the inhabitants of the earth will gloat over them and celebrate and exchange presents, because these two prophets had been a torment to the inhabitants of the earth. But after the three and a half days, the breath of life from God entered them, and they stood on their feet, and those who saw them were terrified.

Narrator: Then they heard a loud voice from heaven saying to them,

Voice: "Come up here!"

Narrator: And they went up to heaven in a cloud while their enemies watched them.

All: At that moment there was a great earthquake, and a tenth of the city fell; seven thousand people were killed in the earthquake, and the rest were terrified and gave glory to the God of heaven. The second woe has passed. The third woe is coming very soon.

Hymn: "Faith Of Our Fathers"

(The narrator moves to the chancel/altar level)

Narrator: Then the seventh angel blew his trumpet, (trumpet fanfare) and there were loud voices in heaven, saying,

All: "The kingdom of the world has become the kingdom of our Lord and of his Messiah, and he will reign forever and ever."

Narrator: Then the 24 elders who sit on their thrones before God fell on their faces and worshiped God, singing,

All: "We give you thanks, Lord God almighty, who are and who were, for you have taken your great power and begun to reign. The nations raged, but your wrath has come, and the time for judging the dead, for rewarding your servants, the prophets and saints and all who fear your name, both small and great, and for destroying those who destroy the earth."

Narrator: Then God's temple in heaven was opened, and the ark of his covenant was seen within his temple; and there were flashes of lightning, rumblings, peals of thunder, an earthquake, and heavy hail.

(Optional) Hymn: "Crown Him with Many Crowns" (under copyright)

(Optional) Musical Interlude: "The Hallelujah Chorus" (all stand)

(Optional 5-minute break)

Act 3 — The War Scroll

Narrator: A great portent appeared in heaven: a woman clothed with the sun, with the moon under her feet, and on her head a crown of twelve stars. She was pregnant and was crying out in birth pangs, in the agony of giving birth. Then another portent appeared in heaven: a great red dragon, with seven heads and ten horns, and seven diadems on his heads. His tail swept down a third of the stars of heaven and threw them to the earth. Then the dragon stood before the woman who was about to bear a child, so that he might devour her child as soon as it was born. And she gave birth to a son, a male child, who is to rule all the nations with a rod of iron. But her child was snatched away and taken to God and to his throne; and the woman fled into the wilderness, where she has a place prepared by God, so that there she can be nourished for 1,260 days. And war broke out in heaven; Michael and his angels fought against the dragon. The dragon and his angels fought back, but they were defeated, and there was no longer any place for them heaven. The great dragon was thrown down, that ancient serpent, who is called the devil and Satan, the deceiver of the whole world — he was thrown down to the earth, and his angels were thrown down with him. Then I heard a loud voice in heaven, proclaiming,

Voice: "Now have come the salvation and the power and the kingdom of our God and the authority of his Messiah, for the accuser of our comrades has been thrown down, who accuses them day and night before our God.

All: But they have conquered him by the blood of the lamb and by the word of their testimony, for they did not cling to life even in the face of death. Rejoice then, you heavens and those who dwell in them! But woe to the earth and the sea, for the devil has come down to you with great wrath, because he knows that his time is short!"

Narrator: So when the dragon saw that he had been thrown down to the earth, he pursued the woman who had given birth to the male child. But the woman was given the two wings of the great eagle, so that she could fly from the serpent into the wilderness, to her place where she is nourished for a time, and times, and half a time. Then from his mouth the serpent poured water like a river after the woman, to sweep her away with the flood. But the earth came to the help of the woman; it opened its mouth and swallowed the river that the dragon had poured from his mouth. Then the dragon was angry with the woman and went off to make war on the rest of her children, those who keep the commandments of God and hold the testimony of Jesus.

(The narrator moves to the congregation level.)

Hymn: "A Mighty Fortress" (verse 1)

Narrator: Then the dragon took his stand on the sand of the seashore. And I saw a beast rising out of the sea having ten horns and seven heads; and on its horns were ten diadems, and on its heads were blasphemous names. And the beast that I saw was like a leopard, its feet were like a bear's, and its mouth was like a lion's mouth. And the dragon gave it his power and his throne and great authority. One of its heads seemed to have received a death-blow, but its mortal wound had been healed. In amazement the whole earth followed the beast. They worshiped the dragon, for he had given his authority to the beast, and they worshiped the beast, saying,

All: "Who is like the beast, and who can fight against it?"

Hymn: "A Mighty Fortress" (verse 2)

Narrator: The beast was given a mouth uttering haughty and blasphemous words, and it was allowed to exercise authority for 42 months. It opened its mouth to utter blasphemies against God, blaspheming his name and his dwelling, that is, those who dwell in heaven. Also it was allowed to make war on the saints and to conquer them. It was given authority over every tribe and people and language and nation, and all the inhabitants of the earth will worship it, everyone whose name has not been written from the foundation of the world in the book of life of the lamb that was slaughtered.

All: Let anyone who has an ear listen: If you are to be taken captive, into captivity you go; if you kill with the sword, with the sword you must be killed. Here is a call for the endurance and faith of the saints.

Hymn: "A Mighty Fortress" (verse 3)

Narrator: Then I saw another beast that rose out of the earth; it had two horns like a lamb and it spoke like a dragon. It exercises all the authority of the first beast on its behalf, and it makes the earth and its inhabitants worship the first beast, whose mortal wound had been healed. It performs great signs, even making fire come down from heaven to earth in the sight of all; and by the signs that it is allowed to perform on behalf of the beast, it deceives the inhabitants of earth, telling them to make an image for the beast that had been wounded by the sword and yet lived; and it was allowed to give breath to the image of the beast so that the image of the beast could even speak and cause those who would not worship the image of the beast to be killed. Also it causes all, both small and great, both rich and poor, both free and slave, to be marked on the right hand or the forehead, so that no one can buy or sell who does not have the mark, that is, the name of the beast or the number of its name.

All: This calls for wisdom: let anyone with understanding calculate the number of the beast, for it is the number of a person. Its number is 666.

Hymn: "A Mighty Fortress" (verse 4)

(The narrator moves to the altar/chancel level)

Narrator: Then I looked, and there was the lamb, standing on Mount Zion!

All: And with him were 144,000 who had his name and his Father's name written on their foreheads.

Narrator: And I heard a voice from heaven like the sound of many waters and like the sound of loud thunder; the voice I heard was like the sound of harpists playing on their harps, and they sing a new song before the throne and before the four living creatures and before the elders. No one could learn that song except the 144,000 who have been redeemed from the earth. It is these who have not defiled themselves with women, for they are virgins; these follow the lamb wherever he goes. They have been redeemed from humankind as first fruits for God and the lamb, and in their mouth no lie was found; they are blameless. Then I saw another angel flying in midheaven, with an eternal gospel to proclaim to those who live on the earth — to every nation and tribe and language and people. He said in a loud voice,

Voice: "Fear God and give him glory, for the hour of his judgment has come; and worship him who made heaven and earth, the sea and the springs of water."

Narrator: Then another angel, a second, followed, saying,

Voice: "Fallen, fallen is Babylon the great! She has made all nations drink of the wine of the wrath of her fornication."

Narrator: Then another angel, a third, followed them, crying with a loud voice.

Voice: "Those who worship the beast and its image, and

receive a mark on their foreheads or on their hands, they will also drink the wine of God's wrath, poured unmixed into the cup of his anger, and they will be tormented with fire and sulfur in the presence of the holy angels and in the presence of the lamb. And the smoke of their torment goes up forever and ever. There is no rest day or night for those who worship the beast and its image and for anyone who receives the mark of its name."

All: Here is a call for the endurance of the saints, those who keep the commandments of God and hold fast to the faith of Jesus.

Narrator: And I heard a voice from heaven saying,

Voice: "Write this: Blessed are the dead who from now on die in the Lord." "Yes," says the Spirit, "they will rest from their labors, for their deeds follow them."

Narrator: Then I looked, and there was a white cloud, and seated on the cloud was one like the Son of Man, with a golden crown on his head, and a sharp sickle in his hand! Another angel came out of the temple, calling with a loud voice to the one who sat on the cloud,

Voice: "Use your sickle and reap, for the hour to reap has come, because the harvest of the earth is fully ripe."

Hymn: "For All The Saints"

(The narrator moves to the congregation level)

Narrator: So the one who sat on the cloud swung his sickle over the earth, and the earth was reaped. Then another angel came out of the temple in heaven, and he too had a sharp sickle. Then another angel came out from the altar, the angel who has authority over fire, and he called with a loud voice to him who had the sharp sickle,

Voice: "Use your sharp sickle and gather the clusters of the vine of the earth, for its grapes are ripe."

Narrator: So the angel swung his sickle over the earth and gathered the vintage of the earth, and he threw it into the great wine press of the wrath of God. And the wine press was trodden outside the city, and blood flowed from the wine press, as high as a horse's bridle, for a distance of about two hundred miles.

Hymn – "Mine Eyes Have Seen The Glory"

Narrator: Then one of the seven angels who had the seven bowls came and said to me,

Voice: "Come, I will show you the judgment of the great whore who is seated on many waters, with whom the kings of the earth have committed fornication, and with the wine of whose fornication the inhabitants of the earth have become drunk."

Narrator: So he carried me away in the spirit into a wilderness, and I saw a woman sitting on a scarlet beast that was full of blasphemous names, and it had seven heads and ten horns. The woman was clothed in purple and scarlet, and adorned with gold and jewels and pearls, holding in her hand a golden cup full of abominations and the impurities of her fornication; and on her forehead was written a name, a mystery:

All: "Babylon the great, mother of whores and of earth's abominations."

Narrator: And I saw that the woman was drunk with the blood of the saints and the blood of the witnesses to Jesus. When I saw her, I was greatly amazed. But the angel said to me,

Voice: "Why are you so amazed? I will tell you the mystery of the woman, and of the beast with seven heads and ten horns that carries her. The beast that you saw was, and is not, and is about to ascend from the bottomless pit and go to destruction. And the inhabitants of the earth, whose names have not been written in the book of life from the foundation of the world, will be amazed when they see the beast, because it was and is not and is to come. This calls for a mind that has wisdom: the seven heads are seven mountains on which the woman is seated; also, they are seven kings, of whom five have fallen, one is living, and the other has not yet come; and when he comes, he must remain only a little while. As for the beast that was and is not, it is an eighth but it belongs to the seven, and it goes to destruction. And the ten horns that you saw are ten kings who have not yet received a kingdom, but they are to receive authority as kings for one hour, together with the beast. These are united in yielding their power and authority to the beast; they will make war on the lamb, and the lamb will conquer them, for he is Lord of lords and King of kings, and those with him are called and chosen and faithful."

Narrator: And he said to me,

Voice: "The waters that you saw, where the whore is seated, are peoples and multitudes and nations and languages. And the ten horns that you saw, they and the beast will hate the whore; they will make her desolate and naked; they will devour her flesh and burn her up with fire. For God has put it into their hearts to carry out his purpose by agreeing to give their kingdom to the beast, until the words of God will be fulfilled. The woman you saw is the great city that rules over the kings of the earth."

Narrator: After this I saw another angel coming down from heaven, having great authority; and the earth was made bright with his splendor. He called out with a mighty voice,

Voice: "Fallen, fallen is Babylon the great! It has become a dwelling place of demons, a haunt of every foul and hateful bird, a haunt of every foul and hateful beast. For all the nations have drunk of the wine of the wrath of her fornication, and the kings of the earth have committed fornication with her, and the merchants of the earth have grown rich from the power of her luxury."

Narrator: Then I heard another voice from heaven saying,

Voice: "Come out of her, my people, so that you do not take part in her sins, and so that you do not share in her plagues; for her sins are heaped high as heaven, and God has remembered her iniquities.

All: Render to her as she herself has rendered, and repay her double for her deeds; mix a double draught for her in the cup she mixed. As she glorified herself and lived luxuriously, so give her a like measure of torment and grief. Since in her heart she says, 'I rule as a queen; I am no widow, and I will never see grief,' therefore her plagues will come in a single day — pestilence and mourning and famine — and she will be burned with fire; for mighty is the Lord God who judges her."

Narrator: Then a mighty angel took up a stone like a great millstone and threw it into the sea, saying,

Voice: "With such violence Babylon the great city will be thrown down, and will be found no more; and the sound of harpists and minstrels and of flutists and trumpeters will be heard in you no more; and an artisan of any trade will be found in you no more; and the sound of the millstone will be heard in you no more; and the light of a lamp will shine in you no more; and the voice of bridegroom and bride will be heard in you no more; for your merchants were the magnates of the earth, and all nations were deceived by your sorcery.

All: And in you was found the blood of prophets and of saints, and of all who have been slaughtered on earth."

Hymn: "Canticle Of The Turning" (verses 3 and 4)

(The narrator moves to the altar/chancel level)

Narrator: After this I heard what seemed to be the loud voice of a great multitude in heaven, saying,

All: "Hallelujah! Salvation and glory and power to our God, for his judgments are true and just; he has judged the great whore who corrupted the earth with her fornication, and he has avenged on her the blood of his servants."

Narrator: Once more they said,

All: "Hallelujah! The smoke goes up from her forever and ever."

Narrator: And the 24 elders and the four living creatures fell down and worshiped God who is seated on the throne, saying,

All: "Amen. Hallelujah!"

Narrator: And from the throne came a voice saying,

Voice: "Praise our God, all you his servants, and all who fear him, small and great."

Narrator: Then I heard what seemed to be the voice of a great multitude, like the sound of many waters and like the sound of mighty thunderpeals, crying out,

All: "Hallelujah! For the Lord our God the almighty reigns. Let us rejoice and exult and give him the glory, for the marriage of the lamb has come, and his bride has made herself ready; to her it has been granted to be clothed with fine linen, bright and pure"

Narrator: — for the fine linen is the righteous deeds of the saints. And the angel said to me,

Voice: "Write this: Blessed are those who are invited to the marriage supper of the lamb."

Narrator: And he said to me,

Voice: "These are true words of God."

Narrator: Then I fell down at his feet to worship him, but he said to me,

Voice: "You must not do that! I am a fellow servant with you and your comrades who hold the testimony of Jesus. Worship God! For the testimony of Jesus is the spirit of prophecy."

Narrator: Then I saw heaven opened, and there was a white horse! Its rider is called Faithful and True, and in righteousness he judges and makes war. His eyes are like a flame of fire, and on his head are many diadems; and he has a name inscribed that no one knows but himself. He is clothed in a robe dipped in blood, and his name is called The Word of God. And the armies of heaven, wearing fine linen, white and pure, were following him on white horses. From his mouth comes a sharp sword with which to strike down the nations, and he will rule them with a rod of iron; he will tread the wine press of the fury of the wrath of God the almighty. On his robe and on his thigh he has a name inscribed, "King of kings and Lord of lords."

Hymn: "Hallelujah Chorus"

(Narrator moves to the congregation level)

Narrator: Then I saw the beast and the kings of the earth with their armies gathered to make war against the rider on the horse and against his army. And the beast was captured, and with it the false prophet who had performed in its presence the signs by which he deceived those who had received the mark of the beast and those who worshiped its image. These two were thrown alive into the lake of fire that burns with sulfur. And the rest were killed by the sword of the rider on the horse, the sword that came from his mouth; and all the birds were gorged with their flesh. Then I saw an angel coming down from heaven, holding in his hand the key to the bottomless pit and a great chain. He seized the dragon, that ancient serpent, who is the devil and satan, and bound him for a thousand years, and threw him into the pit, and locked and sealed it over him, so that he would deceive the nations no more, until the thousand years were ended. After that he must be let out for a little while.

(Narrator moves back to altar level)

Hymn: "Crown Him With Many Crowns"

Narrator: Then I saw thrones, and those seated on them were given authority to judge. I also saw the souls of those who had been beheaded for their testimony to Jesus and for the word of God. They had not worshiped the beast or its image and had not received its mark on their foreheads or their hands. They came to life and reigned with Christ a thousand years. The rest of the dead did not come to life until the thousand years were ended. This is the first resurrection.

All: Blessed and holy are those who share in the first resurrection. Over these the second death has no power, but they will be priests of God and of Christ, and they will reign with him a thousand years.

Narrator: When the thousand years are ended, Satan will be released from his prison and will come out to deceive the nations at the four corners of the earth, Gog and Magog, in order to gather them for battle; they are as numerous as the sands of the sea. They marched up over the breadth of the earth and surrounded the camp of the saints and the beloved city. And fire came down from heaven and consumed them. And the devil who had deceived them was thrown into the lake of fire and sulfur, where the beast and the false prophet were, and they will be tormented day and night forever and ever. Then I saw a great white throne and the one who sat on it; the earth and the heaven fled from his presence, and no place was found for them. And I saw the dead, great and small, standing before the throne, and books were opened. Also another book was opened, the book of life. And the dead were judged according to their works, as recorded in the books. And the sea gave up the dead that were in it, Death and Hades gave up the dead that were in them, and all were judged according to what they had done. Then Death and Hades were thrown into the lake of fire. This is the second death, the lake of fire; and anyone whose name was not found written in the book of life was thrown into the lake of fire.

Hymn: "Crown Him With Many Crowns" (verse 3)

(Narrator begins to move to congregation level while reading - this is the last movement)

Narrator: Then I saw a new heaven and a new earth; for the first heaven and the first earth had passed away, and the sea was no more. And I saw the holy city, the new Jerusalem, coming down out of heaven from God, prepared as a bride adorned for her husband. And I heard a loud voice from the throne saying,

Voice: "See, the home of God is among mortals. He will dwell with them as their God; they will be his peoples, and God himself will be with them; he will wipe every tear from their eyes. Death will be no more; mourning and crying and pain will be no more, for the first things have passed away."

Narrator: And the one who was seated on the throne said,

Jesus: "See, I am making all things new."

Narrator: Also he said,

Jesus: "Write this, for these words are trustworthy and true."

Narrator: Then he said to me,

Jesus: "It is done! I am the Alpha and the Omega, the beginning and the end. To the thirsty I will give water as a gift from the spring of the water of life. Those who conquer will inherit these things, and I will be their God and they will be my children. But as for the cowardly, the faithless, the polluted, the murderers, the fornicators, the sorcerers, the idolaters, and all liars, their place will be in the lake that burns with fire and sulfur, which is the second death."

Hymn: "Love Divine, All Loves Excelling" (stand) (verses 1 and 4)

Narrator: Then one of the seven angels who had the seven bowls full of the seven last plagues came and said to me,

Voice: "Come, I will show you the bride, the wife of the lamb."

Narrator: And in the spirit he carried me away to a great, high mountain and showed me the holy city Jerusalem coming down out of heaven from God. It has the glory of God and a radiance like a very rare jewel, like jasper, clear as crystal. It has a great, high wall with twelve gates, and at the gates twelve angels, and on the gates are inscribed the names of the twelve tribes of the Israelites; on the east three gates, on the north three gates, on the south three gates, and on the west three gates. And the wall of the city has twelve foundations, and on them are the twelve names of the twelve apostles of the lamb.

Hymn: "For All The Saints"

Narrator: And the twelve gates are twelve pearls, each of the gates is a single pearl, and the street of the city is pure gold, transparent as glass. I saw no temple in the city, for its temple is the Lord God the almighty and the lamb. And the city has no need of sun or moon to shine on it, for the glory of God is its light, and its lamp is the lamb. The nations will walk by its light, and the kings of the earth will bring their glory into it. Its gates will never be shut by day — and there will be no night there. People will bring into it the glory and the honor of the nations. But nothing unclean will enter it, nor anyone who practices abomination or falsehood, but only those who are written in the lamb's book of life.

Narrator: Then the angel showed me the river of the water of life, bright as crystal, flowing from the throne of God and of the lamb through the middle of the street of the city. On either side of the river is the tree of life with its twelve kinds of fruit, producing its fruit each month; and the leaves of the tree are for the healing of the nations. Nothing accursed will be found there anymore. But the throne of God and of the lamb will be in it, and his servants will worship him; they will see his face, and his name will be on their foreheads. And there will be no more night; they need no light of lamp or sun, for the Lord God will be their light, and they will reign forever and ever.

Hymn: "Shall We Gather At The River?"

Narrator: And he said to me,

Voice: "These words are trustworthy and true, for the Lord, the God of the spirits of the prophets, has sent his angel to show his servants what must soon take place."

Jesus: "See, I am coming soon! Blessed is the one who keeps the words of the prophecy of this book."

Narrator: I, John, am the one who heard and saw these things. And when I heard and saw them, I fell down to worship at the feet of the angel who showed them to me; but he said to me,

Voice: "You must not do that! I am a fellow servant with you and your comrades the prophets, and with those who keep the words of this book. Worship God!"

Narrator: And he said to me,

Voice: "Do not seal up the words of the prophecy of this book, for the time is near. Let the evildoer still do evil, and the filthy still be filthy, and the righteous still do right, and the holy still be holy."

Jesus: "See, I am coming soon; my reward is with me, to repay according to everyone's work. I am the Alpha and the Omega, the first and the last, the beginning and the end."

All: Blessed are those who wash their robes, so that they will have the right to the tree of life and may enter the city by the gates.

Narrator: Outside are the dogs and sorcerers and fornicators and murderers and idolaters, and everyone who loves and practices falsehood.

Jesus: "It is I, Jesus, who sent my angel to you with this testimony for the churches. I am the root and the descendant of David, the bright morning star."

Narrator: The Spirit and the bride say, "Come." And let everyone who hears say,

All: "Come."

Narrator: And let everyone who is thirsty come. Let anyone who wishes take the water of life as a gift. I warn everyone who hears the words of the prophecy of this book: if anyone adds to them, God will add to that person the plagues described in this book; if anyone takes away from the words of the book of this prophecy, God will take away that person's share in the tree of life and in the holy city, which are described in this book. The one who testifies to these things says,

Jesus: "Surely I am coming soon."

All: Amen. Come, Lord Jesus!

Narrator: The grace of the Lord Jesus be with all the saints.

All: Amen.

Hymn: "I Want To Walk As A Child Of The Light" (verses 1, 2, and 3)

Afterword

From the beginning, the Christian church has had a love/hate relationship with the book of Revelation. The church has loved Revelation's visions of heaven, the ecstasy of worship before God's throne, the hope for a better world and the healing of the nations. Concurrently, the church has been embarrassed by its violent language, its portrayal of a wrathful God and its graphic depiction of eternal torment in hell. Revelation is like a dysfunctional family member who cannot figure out how to be nice, who suffers from bi-polar disorder with its extreme mood swings. And yet, in spite of all its problems, Revelation is still part of the family, still has an important and needed voice to add to family deliberations.

In the past, many mainline pastors have had the begrudging attitude that this family member is okay to visit once a year, during a reunion. They are relieved when the obligatory visit is over. It is better to let this wild-eyed family member hang out with the crazies.

This attitude is changing around the church. People are discovering that this bizarre family member is really not all that wild, and that once they learn to speak its language, Revelation actually helps them make sense of their world. Once thought to suffer from some form of dementia, Revelation is now seen by some scholars to be one of the smartest and most relevant members of the family for our day.

I believe that there is an openness to engaging the book of Revelation today in significant ways. What preachers need is a resource to give them confidence stepping into the pulpit with the lamb, or with the beast, for that matter. John has a powerful prophetic voice. He is confident and sure of his discernment of the times. We can learn from his example.

The political climate in the US today is increasingly divided. We have a variety of people sitting in our pews listening to our sermons. Sometimes preachers have to exercise great care when it comes to applying Revelation's message to our day. I am more inclined to draw parallels to the recent past in hopes that the congregation itself will apply the message of Revelation to contemporary issues. As Adela Yarbro Collins has so powerfully said, "the church of every age must name the beast."[125] Naming those powers and principalities is often best a communal process of discernment, not a lone voice "crying in the wilderness." Preaching through Revelation, accompanied by a Bible study or adult forum to further engage the congregation, can be both helpful and fruitful.

125 Adela Yarbro Collins, *Crisis and Catharsis: The Power of the Apocalypse* (Philadelphia, PA: Westminster Press, 1984), 175.

Bibliography

Armstrong, John H. "Why Some Christians Still Love Conspiracy
    Theories." Act3Online. http://www.act3online.com/
    ArticlesDetail.asp?id=267 (accessed January 15, 2008).
Baker, Sharon L. *Razing Hell: Rethinking Everything You've Been Taught
    about God's Wrath and Judgment.* Louisville: Westminster John
    Knox Press, 2010.
Barr, David L. "Doing Violence: Moral Issues in Reading John's
    Apocalypse." In *Reading the Book of Revelation: A Resource for
    Students*, ed. David L. Barr, 97-108. Atlanta, GA: Society of
    Biblical Literature, 2003.
Barr, David L. "The Apocalypse of John as Oral Enactment."
    Interpretation 40 (1986): 243-56.
"The Lamb Who Looks Like a Dragon? Characterizing Jesus in John's
    Apocalypse." In *The Reality of Apocalypse: Rhetoric and Politics
    in the Book of Revelation*, ed. David L. Barr, 205-20. Atlanta, GA:
    Society of Biblical Literature, 2006.
Tales of the End: A Narrative Commentary on the Book of Revelation. Santa
    Rosa, CA: Polebridge Press, 1998.
Bartlett, David L. *Between the Bible and the Church: New Methods for
    Biblical Preaching.* Nashville: Abingdon Press, 1999.
Bauckham, Richard. *The Theology of the Book of Revelation.* New
    Testament Theology. New York: Cambridge University Press,
    1993.
Bell, Rob. Love Wins: A Book About Heaven, Hell, and the Fate of
    Every Person Who Ever Lived. New York: HarperCollins, 2011.
Blount, Brian K. *Can I Get a Witness: Reading Revelation through African
    American Culture.* Louisville, KY: Westminster John Knox
    Press, 2005.
Boring, M. Eugene. *Revelation.* Edited by James L. Mays.
    Interpretation, a Bible Commentary for Teaching and
    Preaching. Louisville, KY: John Knox Press, 1989.
Braaten, Mark. *Come, Lord Jesus: A Study of Revelation.* Collegeville,
    MN: Liturgical Press, 2007/2018. the author came out with an
    updated 2nd edition.

Campbell, Charles L. "Apocalypse Now: Preaching Revelation as Narrative." In *Narrative Reading, Narrative Preaching: Reuniting New Testament Interpretation and Proclamation*, ed. Joel B. Green and Michael Pasquarello, 151-75. Grand Rapids, MI: Baker Academic, 2003.

Carey, Greg. "Teaching and Preaching the Book of Revelation in the Church." *Review & Expositor* 98.1 (2001): 87-100.

Collins, Adela Yarbro. *Crisis and Catharsis: The Power of the Apocalypse*. Philadelphia, PA: Westminster Press, 1984.

Dawn, Marva J. *Joy in Our Weakness: A Gift of Hope from the Book of Revelation*. Rev. ed. Grand Rapids, MI: Wm. B. Eerdmans Publishing Co., 2002.

Farmer, Ronald L. *Revelation*. Edited by Russell Pregeant and David J. Lull. Chalice Commentaries for Today. St. Louis, MO: Chalice Press, 2005.

Fee, Gordon D. "Preaching Apocalyptic? You've Got to Be Kidding!" *Calvin Theological Journal* 41.1 (2006): 7-16.

Gonzalez, Catherine. "Mission Accomplished; Mission Begun: Lent and the Book of Revelation." *Journal for Preachers* 32.2 (1999): 9-13.

Howard-Brook, Wes, and Anthony Gwyther. *Unveiling Empire: Reading Revelation Then and Now*. The Bible & Liberation Series. Maryknoll, NY: Orbis Books, 1999.

Jacobsen, David Schnasa. *Preaching in the New Creation: The Promise of New Testament Apocalyptic Texts*. Louisville, KY: Westminster John Knox Press, 1999.

Jones, Larry Paul, and Jerry L. Sumney. *Preaching Apocalyptic Texts*. St. Louis, MO: Chalice Press, 1999.

Just, Felix. "Art, Images, Music and Materials Related to the Book of Revelation." Catholic-Resources.org. http://catholic-resources.org/Art/Revelation-Art.htm (accessed January 13, 2008).

Kirsch, Jonathan. *A History of the End of the World: How the Most Controversial Book in the Bible Changed the Course of Western Civilization*. San Francisco, CA: HarperSanFrancisco, 2006.

Koester, Craig R. *Revelation and the End of All Things*. Grand Rapids, MI: Wm. B. Eerdmans Publishing Co., 2001.

Koester, Craig R. *Revelation*. The Anchor Yale Bible, vol. 38A. New
	Haven, CT: Yale University Press, 2014.

Kovacs, Judith, and Christopher Rowland. *Revelation: The Apocalypse of
	Jesus Christ*. Edited by John Sawyer, Christopher Rowland and
	Judith Kovacs. Blackwell Bible Commentaries. Malden, MA:
	Blackwell Publishing, 2004.

LaHaye, Tim, and Jerry Jenkins. *Left Behind: A Novel of the Earth's Last
	Days*. Wheaton, IL: Tyndale House Publishers, 1996.

Lawrence, D. H. *Apocalypse*. London: Heinemann, 1931.

Lose, David J. "What Does This Mean? A Four-Part Exercise in
	Reading Mark 9:2-9 (Transfiguration)." *Word & World* 23.1
	(2003): 85-93.

Maier, Harry O. *Apocalypse Recalled: The Book of Revelation after
	Christendom*. Minneapolis, MN: Fortress Press, 2002.

McClaren, Brian D. *The Last Word and the Word After That: A Tale of
	Faith, Doubt, and a New Kind of Christianity*. San Francisco:
	Jossey-Bass, 2005.

Norris, Kathleen. "Introduction." In *Revelation*, ed. Will Self, 1-12.
	New York: Grove Press, 1999.

O'Day, Gail R. "Teaching and Preaching the Book of Revelation."
	Word & World 25.3 (2005): 246-54.

Pagels, Elaine. *Revelations: Visions, Prophecy, & Politics in the Book of
	Revelation.* New York: Viking Penguin, 2012.

Pilgrim, Walter E. *Uneasy Neighbors: Church and State in the New
	Testament*. Overtures to Biblical Theology. Minneapolis, MN:
	Fortress Press, 1999.

Quanbeck II, Philip A. "Preaching Apocalyptic Texts." *Word & World*
	25.3 (2005): 317-27.

Rhoads, David. "Introduction." In *From Every People and Nation: The
	Book of Revelation in Intercultural Perspective*, ed. David Rhoads,
	1-27. Minneapolis, MN: Augsburg Fortress Press, 2005.

Rossing, Barbara R. *Journeys Through Revelation: Apocalyptic Hope for
	Today*. Presbyterian Women, Inc., 2010.

Rossing, Barbara R. *The Rapture Exposed: The Message of Hope in the
	Book of Revelation*. Boulder, CO: Westview Press, 2004.

Rossing, Barbara R. "The World is About to Turn: Preaching Apocalyptic Texts for a Planet in Peril," In *Eco-Reformation: Grace and Hope for a Planet in Peril*, ed. Lisa E. Dahill, Jim B. Martin-Schramm Wipf and Stock Publishers, 2016.

Saunders, Stanley P. "Revelation and Resistance: Narrative and Worship in John's Apocalypse." In *Narrative Reading, Narrative Preaching: Reuniting New Testament Interpretation and Proclamation*, ed. Joel B. Green and Michael Pasquarello, 117-50. Grand Rapids, MI: Baker Academic, 2003.

Schüssler Fiorenza, Elisabeth. *Revelation: Vision of a Just World*. Proclamation Commentaries. Minneapolis, MN: Fortress Press, 1991.

Spilsbury, Paul. *The Throne, the Lamb & the Dragon: A Reader's Guide to the Book of Revelation*. Downers Grove, IL: InterVarsity Press, 2002.

Stendahl, Krister. "Biblical Theology, Contemporary." In *The Interpreter's Dictionary of the Bible*, ed. George Buttrick et al, 418-31. Nashville: Abingdon, 1962.

Wilson, Mark. *Charts on the Book of Revelation: Literary, Historical, and Theological Perspectives*. Grand Rapids: Kregel Publications, 2007.

Wink, Walter. *The Powers That Be: Theology for a New Millennium*. New York: Doubleday, 1998.

With increasing interest in apocalyptic themes in light of recent events, Pastor Rolf Svanoe has written *The Beast in the Pulpit* with a goal of "providing a resource for preachers to engage the latest research and insights into Revelation." Because this book of the Bible is often misread and misrepresented in media, it is essential that Christians are able to explore the true intent and story within John's writing of Revelation.

"The preacher's task is to discern the main thought or point and then teach it in a way that people can apply to their lives." In order to accomplish this in the book of Revelation, Svanoe has performed a close reading of each chapter throughout his book, helping readers to understand what these phrases meant when they were written, and what they mean for modern readers.

In his final chapters, Svanoe has structured a dramatic reading of Revelation, allowing for up to four actors to portray the events in front of a congregation for ease of comprehension. This book is written for all of God's children, to help clarify this daunting book at the end of the Bible. Whether you have read Revelation over and over or never at all, you are sure to learn something from *The Beast in the Pulpit*.

Author Bio for Rolf D. Svanoe

Rolf Svanoe is a recently retired ELCA pastor living in Decorah, Iowa. During his 36 years of ministry, he served congregations in Wisconsin, South Dakota and Minnesota. A graduate of Augustana University and Luther Seminary, he earned his Doctor of Ministry degree in 2008.

www.ingramcontent.com/pod-product-compliance
Lightning Source LLC
Chambersburg PA
CBHW021402090426
42742CB00009B/962